Schools That Succeed, Students Who Achieve

Profiles of Programs Helping All Students to Learn

James Deneen

ROWMAN & LITTLEFIELD EDUCATION

A division of

ROWMAN & LITTLEFIELD PUBLISHERS, INC.
Lanham • *New York* • *Toronto* • *Plymouth, UK*

Published by Rowman & Littlefield Education
A division of Rowman & Littlefield Publishers, Inc.
A wholly owned subsidary of The Rowman & Littlefield Publishing Group, Inc.
4501 Forbes Boulevard, Suite 200, Lanham, Maryland 20706
http://www.rowmaneducation.com

Estover Road
Plymouth PL6 7PY
United Kingdom

British Library Cataloguing in Publication Information Available

Library of Congress Cataloging-in-Publication Data

Deneen, James R.
   Schools that succeed, students who achieve : profiles of programs helping all students
to learn / James Deneen.
      p. cm.
   Includes bibliographical references.
   ISBN 978-1-60709-340-4 (cloth : alk. paper) — ISBN 978-1-60709-341-1 (pbk. : alk.
paper) — ISBN 978-1-60709-342-8 (electronic)
   1. School improvement programs—United States.   2. Academic achievement—
United States. I. Title.
   LB2822.82.D46 2010
   371.2'070973—dc22   2009031907

Printed in the United States of America

©™ The paper used in this publication meets the minimum requirements of American
National Standard for Information Sciences—Permanence of Paper for Printed Library
Materials, ANSI/NISO Z39.48-1992.

I dedicate this book to Thalia, Chris, and Val, my great supporters and constant joy.

Contents

Preface

When principals and teachers hear of programs in other schools that substantially improve student achievement, they usually ask several questions:

- Does this program or intervention really work? What is the evidence for its success?
- Does it work in schools and classes like mine? That is, are the students in the successful school at the same achievement level as mine, and does this school have resources that are not available to my school?

These are sensible questions to pose before even considering adopting a new program in any class or school. They are the rationale for this book, which describes many schools that have demonstrated an ability to lift their students' academic achievement. In separate chapters, this book looks at elementary, middle, and high schools. We describe the principal characteristics of each school, especially the academic achievement levels and, where available, the growth of students over several years. We also indicate the resources available to the profiled schools for realizing such growth, and the problems they have overcome.

Our focus in this process is on helping faculty to identify programs that are effective in schools that resemble their own. Our hope is that, having identified one or several promising interventions, administrators and teachers will gather more detailed information about schools and programs they have identified. For any major intervention, the principal and faculty may wish to contact the exemplary schools directly, and even visit them to observe firsthand the characteristics of the schools and the program. At that time, the visitors could discuss with administrators and teachers what is needed to begin and maintain such a program. The visiting faculty can then decide whether the successful programs seem applicable to their school; if the decision is favorable, they can begin planning how to implement the intervention in their school.

A belief that change is possible is a prerequisite for bringing about change. That positive attitude is difficult to maintain when, on the basis of test scores or graduation rates, a school ranks low in relation to other local or state schools and is threatened with sanctions for unsatisfactory student achievement. School staff may feel that much of the cause of unsatisfactory student achievement is beyond their control, and they are being required to do the impossible.

A common response to poor results on state assessments is to intensify test preparation sessions. If these sessions are related to the standards and curriculum that the assessment measures, the sessions can be productive of real learning and better test scores. If in test preparation classes, teachers simply review old test items, or spend more than a brief period on test-taking techniques, the hours taken from the curriculum are not being used productively.

Besides having confidence in the possibility for upgrading student achievement, principals and teachers must be willing to undertake the hard work necessary to achieve results from a substantial curriculum change. For teachers, that may mean extensive professional development to upgrade their content knowledge, and to learn new strategies for teaching. Innovative programs need time to work. Despite occasional reports of very large one-year gains in reading, for example, upgrading and maintaining students' reading skills is usually a multi-year project. Over that period, teachers will invest in professional development that upgrades their content knowledge, as well as learning new teaching strategies.

Initially, some experienced teachers may be unenthusiastic about more professional development, having sat through too many lectures during "Professional Development Days" that resulted in little learning and few changes in classroom teaching. They have seen programs proposed as panaceas dwindle and die. The professional development that serious curriculum change calls for cannot be a one-shot program with consultants lecturing and a few small-group activities. Substantive improvement of teachers' professional knowledge and skills demands ongoing sessions in a variety of formats over an extended period. To remain vital, professional development that serious curriculum change requires must be more than one or a few sessions with lectures and brief activities. To be successful, professional development must be planned by teachers and administrators together and include ongoing cooperative learning as teachers try out the activities and strategies in classrooms, then cooperatively evaluate and improve upon them.

We believe teachers' knowledge of positive changes achieved by other schools with student populations like theirs can kindle a positive response to changes in their own classrooms. Once a need has been identified, principals and teachers can develop a plan for their school that includes needed resources, a schedule of implementation, and other obvious features. A critical element in such a plan is the professional development activities teachers will need; another is a decision on how the program will be evaluated.

Our text consists of two major parts. The first section, "Problems," considers several basic questions related to raising student achievement. These issues include differences among educators on just what students should learn, what state, national, and international assessments tell us about the status of U.S. students' academic knowledge and skills, and whether transferring successful practices from one school to another is feasible.

The second part of this book, solutions, presents profiles of schools that have demonstrated their ability to raise their students' achievement significantly. We divide the chapters by elementary, middle, and high schools, and profile schools from extremely poor to very affluent communities, with greater emphasis on schools that have achieved notable success with economically disadvantaged students. With each school described, we indicate demographic characteristics of the school and its community, the evidence that it has a considerable impact on its students' academic learning, and the programs and resources that appear to lead to the schools' exceptional performance.

The text's final two chapters speak to the importance of and processes for evaluating curriculum changes, and offer recommendations for implementing curricular change and improving student achievement. The book concludes with a glossary, references, and websites for identifying successful schools.

Part I

Problems

Before looking at possible solutions to U.S. students' problems with academic achievement, let's try to understand the problems.

One difficulty arises from educators' disagreement over what constitutes academic achievement. This divergence may be described as "content versus process" or "traditional versus progressive." Obviously, differences in what students should be learning have implications for what they are taught and what they do learn. Those espousing either position can agree on the importance of at least minimal literacy in language and mathematics, although they differ on how that learning should be acquired (see chapter one).

Another series of problems arises from trying to determine the status of academic achievement in the U.S.: how well are our students now learning? A simple measure is the average of U.S. students' achievement scores on tests of math, language, and science when compared with those of their peers in their countries. Such comparisons offer important information, but they can also be misleading. National averages between highly disparate student populations are too simplistic a basis to provide satisfactory and definitive answers to our questions about U.S. students' academic achievement. Nor can such comparisons explain why some student populations achieve notably better than others; thus they provide little guidance regarding what to do about the disparities.

Countrywide averages don't inform us about the performance of subgroups within each nation's student population, including the most economically and educationally disadvantaged, and the more fortunate and gifted students. Another difficulty arises from comparing students in Hong Kong, which has a fairly homogenous population of seven million, with those in the U.S, with its 300 million-plus population and highly diverse 50 million students (see chapter two).

1

Another question that bears on the subject of this book is why more schools don't imitate those that are successful (discussed in chapter three). We know there are schools at every grade level that have overcome barriers to learning and demonstrated that students at all levels of achievement can improve, sometimes dramatically.

Perhaps many principals and teachers don't know about these high-achieving schools. Others may believe, sometimes with good reason, that these successful schools don't suffer from the problems that afflict them. We hope this book helps to remedy a lack of information, and offers reassurance that schools that "look like my school" are providing the knowledge and skills that all teachers want their students to master.

Chapter 1

Great Expectations: What Should All Students Learn?

SETTING STANDARDS

Standards, the byword of the current decade, are what state and local educators believe students should learn in school. Curricula drawn from these standards and assessed in state testing programs attempt to measure the concepts, knowledge, and skills students have learned.

Some critics of state standards point out that the standards themselves, as well as curricula and tests derived from them, can overemphasize factual knowledge, learning that lends itself to multiple-choice and short-answer testing. To the extent this objection points out a limitation of many current state assessments, it deserves consideration; in several states, test developers are trying new item types that tap more complex skills without an unacceptable loss of reliability and efficiency. Nevertheless, a great deal of what students need to learn falls into the category of information; current assessments that are well designed and focus on important rather than trivial knowledge are important indicators of student achievement.

The Introduction to History-Social Science Content Standards for California Public Schools (California Department of Education, 2000) illustrates the standards-to-specifics problem in determining and measuring what students should learn. For grade three, Standard 3.4 reads, "Discuss the importance of public virtue and the role of citizens, including how to participate in a classroom, in the community, and in civic life" (p. 10). *Discuss* is not a process that most third grade teachers find very productive if students are expected to bring much background knowledge to bear in the discussion. *Public virtue* and *the role of citizens* are vague phrases likely to generate blank stares from eight-year-olds. Third graders should surely learn how to participate in a

3

classroom, but encouraging them to analogize their classroom responsibilities to the community and civic life seems premature. The difficulty in teaching this standard is matched by the problem a test writer would have in devising appropriate questions to determine how well students had mastered it.

To those who subscribe to the readin,' writin' and 'rithmetic curriculum, the answer to "What should students be expected to learn?" seems obvious. But even a teacher committed to basic knowledge and skills as the cornerstone of schooling would agree that students must also learn social and behavioral norms not only at home, but in school; without them, little learning of language, math, science, art, and other disciplines will occur. Be aware that when student learning is mentioned in this text, we refer primarily to the academic subjects like those mentioned above. Academic learning is the core function of a school. So, our response to the question at the head of this chapter is "From the earliest school years, all students should learn to read, write, speak, and listen in increasingly complex ways, as well as to progress from basic arithmetic to complex mathematical learning." And we add that, in every grade through high school, students should become increasingly capable of using the tools of language and math as they master steadily more demanding knowledge and skills in science, social studies, and other important subjects.

Some who agree with these objectives may protest that they omit the social skills and emotional development that are critically important for student learning, beginning in preschool and the earliest elementary grades and continuing through the high school years. Let's agree that teachers must do all they can to encourage and inculcate norms of self-control and appropriate interactions with others. When students possess these skills, they are ready to be taught and to learn. Youngsters who lack these skills and behaviors have difficulty concentrating on a task and disrupt the focus of others.

This text does not list social and emotional development among the *primary* curriculum goals of a school. Certainly, they are important, but the school's responsibility for teaching them is secondary to the obligation of parents to prepare their children for school learning by patiently indoctrinating and reinforcing the norms of acceptable behavior. Unfortunately, some parents can't or simply don't instill appropriate standards of interacting with others, or help their children develop healthy control of their emotions.

A number of schools have successfully taken over these obligations when parents have been unable to fulfill them. These schools regulate how students dress, how they behave within and sometimes outside the school, how their homework should be monitored, and other elements of their students' lives. They prescribe in detail what is and is not acceptable in students' interactions with teachers, other adults, and fellow students.

More credit to the teachers and principals who patiently assume the difficult task of training students to behave in ways that permit them and others to learn. In the best of worlds, these time- and energy-draining tasks would not fall to the schools. In any case, the school's primary goal, the one for which it is best suited, is to help students master the information and skills that will enable them to continue to learn and to become independent, productive adults.

Our statements about what students should learn in school basically agree with Frey and her colleagues (Frey, 2005, p. 10). She lists three sets of essential knowledge and skills: content-area knowledge, social skills and habits of mind, and communication skills.

Frey's *content knowledge* suggests the importance of knowledge for acquiring further learning. The tools of computer science, the alignment of places, dates, people, and events that underlies progress in studying history, or the vocabulary, grammar, and literary forms one needs to read beyond simple decoding, all point to prior knowledge as a requisite for future learning. Comprehension demands context and structure, so traditional educators favor adhering to a prescribed curriculum and lesson plans. Every lesson should be followed, and often preceded by at least a brief assessment, so teachers know what has been learned and what needs to be taught.

We reiterate that language knowledge and skills are by far the most fundamental areas of content knowledge. This learning begins in the primary grades with the mechanics of reading, decoding skills, and the like. The skills are constantly buttressed by contextual knowledge and vocabulary building that enable a shift from learning how to read, to reading for substantive knowledge. That shift is accompanied by increasing attention to grammar and syntax, and to the reading of literature and poetry. In later elementary, middle, and high school years, schools also emphasize writing, oral, and aural skills. Frey's *social skills and habits of mind* are precisely the social and emotional development we advocate, and her *communication skills* seem to spread across both content and social learning.

TWO PHILOSOPHIES OF EDUCATION

The Traditionalists

Currently, one of the best known advocates of a traditional approach to schooling that emphasizes teaching knowledge, information, and facts, is E. D. Hirsch, Jr. In his 2006 book, *The Knowledge Deficit*, Hirsch insists that to understand spoken or written language, we need to comprehend the words in a specific text; we then infer meaning from the text by calling on relevant background knowledge that provides a context for the spoken or written message (p. 39). In other words, to read effectively at all levels of schooling, students need a strong vocabulary base, and a context of general information largely derived from reading and, especially for young learners, from listening to others read to them. (For more on the importance of context, see Robert Marzano, 2004.)

Hirsch's ideas on curriculum have been developed into the Core Knowledge texts for the principal subjects in K–8. Core Knowledge has recently been chosen for a pilot program in grades K–2 in 10 New York City public schools (Gootman, August 26, 2008). The pilot study will emphasize reading instruction, and represents a departure from that school system's current reading program, called "Balanced Literacy." Core Knowledge and Balanced Literacy represent the principles of traditional and more progressive approaches to the teaching of reading.

The late Clifton Fadiman succinctly described the purpose of schooling on which Hirsch's principle rests: "The primary job of the school is the efficient transmission and continued reappraisal of what we call tradition" (Fadiman, 1959 p. vii). By tradition, Fadiman refers to the means by which the present learns from the past. For more information on the importance of content and background information, see *Building Background Knowledge for Academic Achievement* (Marzano, 2004).

Progressive Educators

Progressive educators disagree with Fadiman and Hirsch. All learning is ultimately self-learning, argue advocates of a progressive philosophy. That is, one hasn't really *learned* something until that knowledge or skill has been internalized and understood in a way that allows the learner to use it, to apply it in similar or differing contexts.

Thus, the process by which learning is acquired is as important as its subject-content; to a considerable extent, the process *is* the content. A second emphasis in progressive thought is the need for schools to focus on the whole child. There is no point, progressives argue, in trying to pour facts into young minds when the intended receptacles are physically, emotionally, or socially unready to grasp them. Memorization and other teacher-dictated learning tasks should be kept to a minimum; traditionalists' attempts to graft knowledge from the past on to young minds are considered largely futile.

John Dewey is the godfather of progressive educators, especially those in the United States. Dewey is a towering figure in education, and many favored terms and principles of progressive education are associated with him: problem-solving methodologies, child-centered schooling, collaborative learning, learning by doing, and the importance of integrating social justice into the school curriculum.

Dewey's prolific writing during the first half of the 20th century continues to influence U.S. schools of education, and makes him a lightning rod for the criticism of traditional educators. But Dewey's principles had considerable exposure well before his time. Educational philosophers like Rousseau and Pestalozzi, and in the 20th century, Piaget contributed to the view that children's intellectual growth is a process comparable to that of their physical and emotional development. By *development,* these thinkers imply a gradual unfolding of qualities of mind that are essentially innate, as opposed to training or other terms that imply a transfer of knowledge.

This brief review of traditional versus progressive philosophies of education doesn't nearly do justice to the nuances of each position. It intends only to highlight how theories of learning and child development influence answers to our question, "What should students be expected to learn?" Probably all but the most hard-line, true believers in either the traditionalist or progressive camps can perceive at least something, and perhaps a great deal to agree with in the opposing position. Traditionalists, for example, subscribe to the importance of students *using* the knowledge they gain; progressives would surely agree that students must commit certain vocabulary, rules, and processes to memory if they are to learn to read or work with arithmetic.

Our point here is not to reconcile two philosophies, although we'll make some attempts to do so when we consider specific curricula. As ensuing chapters will iterate, in schooling, one size does not fit all; no single philosophy of teaching works always and everywhere. Learning depends of the ability of schools and their teachers to adjust instruction to the specific needs of various groups of students who are at specific levels of achievement. A third grader who struggles with basic decoding, lacks fundamental background knowledge, cannot follow directions, or cannot sit still needs a particular content and method of instruction. Conversely, third graders with a broad background of knowledge from home and previous schooling who read and are comfortable listening to adults speak and read, and who possess at least minimal social controls will be bored and their readiness to learn can be wasted by the type of instruction their less-fortunate peers need.

SOCIAL AND EMOTIONAL LEARNING

Let's return briefly to the non-cognitive learning that children need to succeed in school. Social and emotional controls at some level are surely indispensable if students are to master academic knowledge and skills. Observation in and beyond schooling demonstrates that, without these attributes, children will fail not only in academic courses, but will lead unhappy and isolated lives in school and probably in later life. As mentioned above, social skills, emotional control, and habits of attention and respect for others should first be inculcated in children's earliest years at home, with patient repetition and one-on-one contact with parents as well as with other adults and children. When this early training is at least minimally effective, preschool and primary grade teachers can further help their young charges develop these habits. Success in these efforts depends on teachers having the knowledge and time to devise training that is appropriate to the successive stages of children's cognitive and physical growth.

The time and effort that school personnel should expend on helping students to mature socially and emotionally varies according to the extent students bring these qualities from extra-school environments. But these qualities will always be a part of every school's curriculum, if only because classrooms, playgrounds, and athletic fields elicit social and emotional responses specific to those environments. Nevertheless, we insist that intellectual growth is the school's primary task; students' health, social progress, and emotional development are requisites that allow the school to carry out its most essential function.

The opinion just expressed may not sound much like Dewey's principle of educating the whole child. In fact, schools do contribute in some degree to all aspects of their students' lives; children don't bring only their cognitive faculties into a classroom. Nevertheless, our purpose in this text is simply to focus on the principal task of schools—the academic knowledge and skills at which they are best equipped to succeed. When a curriculum loses that concentration, learning can begin to focus narrowly on processes like team building, class projects, and other student-directed activities. That is not an argument for students sitting in rows of desks, listening while a teacher delivers large chunks of information to them. In fact, even the most disciplined and orderly students will not long attend to poor teaching. Both traditional and progressive curricula can be presented badly; both can be made interesting. But the differing learning theories of content versus process are the bases for answering our query about what students should learn, and thus of school curriculum in the U.S. today.

SUMMARY

Standards express what educators believe students should know and be able to do. Curriculum developers are handicapped by vague or overly general standards; test developers tend toward factual items that assess basic cognitive levels, such as defining and comprehending. Such knowledge is an important but partial element of student learning.

Traditional curricula emphasize intensive early training in basic language studies and mathematics. This approach stresses the mechanics of learning to read, especially phonics, and the importance of memorization and vocabulary building. A wide range of background knowledge is considered necessary for reading comprehension. This heavy weighting of academic content is the primary, but not the sole objective of the curriculum; self-control and social skills are prerequisites for learning.

Progressive educators view the process—learning to learn—more than the subject content as the essence of a K–12 curriculum. Progressive educators also urge more strongly than their traditionalist colleagues that schools must give high priority to student learning that is not only or even primarily intellectual, but includes physical, social, and emotional goals. This learning is not simply dispositive, as traditionalists say, but is the primary objective of the curriculum. Progressive educators urge that schools educate the *whole* child.

Chapter 2

What the Numbers Tell Us

In deciding what and how to teach, numbers count. We look first at figures that describe U.S. schools and students, and how they affect curriculum and student achievement. Second, we compare achievement levels of U.S. students with those of other countries, and among students within individual States of the U.S. Third, we examine the impact of the first two factors and suggest appropriate interpretations of student scores on international and national testing programs.

DEMOGRAPHICS

Schooling in the United States from kindergarten through 12th grade is a large-scale enterprise. Some 3.3 million teachers and instructional aides are employed in the U.S.'s 15,000 school districts. About 87 percent of these are in public schools.

More than 55 million children are enrolled in 100,000 public or independent U.S. schools; several million more are home schooled. In their homes, one in five students speaks a language other than English. Of these, 10 percent are enrolled in English as a Second Language classes, a 60 percent increase in the ten-year period 1995–2005.

Some 41 percent of students in public school systems receive free or reduced fee lunch, a common metric for defining children of poverty. The effects of severe poverty on student achievement can scarcely be exaggerated. For example, students from families with annual incomes of $10,000 to $20,000 score an average of 443 on the SAT verbal portion, and 463 in mathematics (on a 200 to 800 scale). Students from families with incomes of

11

$100,000 or more average 554 on the verbal and 565 on the math sections of the SAT.

Paul Tough's book *Whatever It Takes* vividly describes the corrosive effects of severe poverty on children's ability to learn, and the extraordinary efforts required to help parents learn how to prepare their young children to succeed in school (Tough, 2008).

One quarter of U.S. third graders have attended two schools since the first grade; for children from low-income families, the mobility factor is tripled. Among third graders who change schools frequently, 41 percent read below grade level, compared with 26 percent who do not change schools. The figures about U.S. school children are drawn from the website of the National Council for Educational Statistics (NCES).

The statistics listed above should provide a yellow warning light: proceed with caution as we study U.S. curricula and assessment procedures and compare them with those of other nations. Some reasons for careful interpretations are these:

• The U.S. student population differs in several respects from those of Finland or Japan, two countries whose students score at the top of international exams. In terms of the size of their student populations versus that of the U.S., the differences are very large.
  The variations are qualitative as well. In the United States, extreme differences in wealth exist, especially between the wealthiest suburbs and the poorest areas of our inner cities. Because community and parental affluence correlate positively and poverty correlates negatively with academic achievement, the variations in wealth are reflected more in U.S. students' achievement than in countries with fewer variations in community and household income.
• The key factor in early learning is language acquisition. One in five U.S. children are raised in homes in which English is not the primary language. Many more children have parents who do not have the resources to read or listen to them, to talk with them, or otherwise encourage a sense of language structure and vocabulary; these youngsters are considerably handicapped as they enter school. Unless promptly remedied, the effects of this deficit surface early, become more severe in middle school, and have devastating effects in high school.
• Lacking a uniform national curriculum, U.S. schools reflect variations among and within our 50 states. The mobility pattern of students' families, especially among the poor, virtually guarantees that students experience breaks in their curricula as they change schools. In logically developed

subjects like mathematics, these gaps can be devastating to achievement and intensely discouraging to students.

- Perhaps most importantly, U.S. families and communities vary widely in how they value and support educational excellence. Certain countries are famous, (some would say infamous), for the heavy community and parental pressure they exert on students to excel in their classes and examinations. Of course, some parents in the U.S. also strongly emphasize study, monitor homework, confer with teachers, own and read books, restrict television and recreational computer time, and make clear their expectations that their children will enter and do well in college and beyond. Such parents are the norm in high-achieving student populations like those of Korea or Singapore.

COMPARISONS OF STUDENT ACHIEVEMENT

Three International Assessments

The fact that U.S. students, unlike their peers in other countries, do not study a curriculum common to all states and school districts encourages caution in assessing their performance on a common test. The three international measures described below are well-designed programs that attempt to focus on subject-matter essentials common to all the curricula, but some variations in content among various national curricula and among U.S. school districts are inevitable. Still, these international assessments offer important information about standards within the subjects tested, and the relative achievement of students around the world.

Trends in International Mathematics and Science Study (TIMSS)

TIMSS examines student achievement in math and science in grades four and eight. In the 2007 assessment cycle, 36 countries in grade four and 48 countries in grade eight participated. The tests are traditional, content-oriented exams; approximately 40 percent of the items are constructed responses, and 60 percent are in a multiple-choice format.

The 2007 assessment results show that fourth grade students in Hong Kong and eighth grade students in Taipei are the top scorers in math, while Singapore has the highest scores in science at both grade levels. American fourth and eighth grade students show solid progress in the most recent examinations; U.S. fourth graders averaged 529 in mathematics, which is higher than the TIMSS scale average of 500.

In Singapore, Taiwan, and Korea, nearly 50 percent of students scored at the advanced levels of mathematics, compared with just six percent in the U.S.

For the 2007 TIMSS survey, the states of Massachusetts and Minnesota participated in a separately funded study. Those two states are making concerted efforts to upgrade their schools' teaching of math and science. Apparently, their efforts are successful, for students in those states demonstrate excellent achievement, outperforming their peers in the U.S. and in all but a handful of other countries.

Program in International Reading Literacy Study (PIRLS)

PIRLS is administered every five years to fourth graders in some 40 countries. Besides the traditional measures of reading skills, the program asks each country's respondents such questions as: "Do fourth graders value and enjoy reading?" "Do students' homes foster reading development?" "How is early reading instruction organized?"

In the 2006 testing cycle, the highest ranking nation was the Russian Federation, with Hong Kong and Singapore in second and third place, respectively. The U.S. placed 18th among the 40 participants.

Program for International Student Assessment (PISA)

PISA is sponsored by the Organization for Economic Cooperation and Development (OECD). The test is administered to 15-year-olds, that is, those nearing the end of compulsory schooling in most countries. So not all test takers are at the same grade level. PISA assesses reading, mathematics, science, literacy, and problem solving. In its fourth cycle of assessment in 2009, PISA will test between 4500–10,000 students in some 62 countries.

Unlike TIMSS and PIRLS, which assess the *presence* of traditional curricular knowledge and skills, PISA focuses on the *use* of knowledge and skills, the application of competencies in real-world contexts. The assessment data are supplemented by a background questionnaire completed by students and principals.

In the last PISA assessment cycle (2006), students in Finland had the highest average score, with Hong Kong in second place, followed by Canada, Taipei, and Estonia. The U.S. ranked 27th, well behind comparable nations like France, Germany, and the United Kingdom.

When the Pisa scores were compared with the questionnaire item on the role of parents and the home, a strong positive correlation emerged for grade four between students' reading achievement and the extent to which parents engaged their preschool age children in early literacy activities. These activities include reading books, telling stories, singing songs, playing with alphabet toys, and word games.

Interpreting International Assessments

Before we examine assessments that focus solely on U.S. students, let's consider what the international programs tell us. We begin with the factors described earlier, which point to the differences between the U.S. student population and those of most other nations. Briefly, those factors are:

1. The quantitative and qualitative differences between U.S. and other student populations.
2. Early language acquisition: when students do not hear and speak English in their homes or when parents cannot foster early language skills, students are handicapped upon entering school. It should be noted, however, that Singapore's high scoring students are largely taught and tested in English, although it is not the native language of most Singaporeans.
3. Variations in curriculum among states' and school districts' disadvantage U.S. students, especially those who transfer schools.
4. Family and community esteem for academic achievement, which is generally higher and more uniform in high-scoring countries than in the U.S.

These factors surely contribute to the mediocre rankings of U.S. students on international assessments. But citing explanations for our undistinguished standings doesn't change the hard fact that *on average,* our students are not learning as much reading, writing, math, or science as their peers in many other nations.

This unfavorable comparison is relatively recent; a few decades ago, U.S. students were among the top scorers in international competitions. One cause for the shift in rankings is the efforts other nations have made to upgrade their curricula, teaching methodologies, and teacher training, changes that have yielded dramatically improved academic performance.

But researchers also point to a leveling off or decline in U.S. students' achievement, beginning about 1980 (Goldin and Katz, 2008). Those authors point out that the beginning of an achievement decline in K–12 schools coincides with a rapidly widening gap in U.S. families' income.

Another factor that surely contributes to the recent surge in student achievement in some countries is their stress on the selection and training of their teachers. Singapore mandates 100 hours of professional development annually for teachers, plus setting aside periods in the school week for cooperative planning with colleagues. Sweden provides 15 days a year for teachers' in-service activities.

These nations and several others that lead in student achievement are highly selective in admitting students into teacher preparation. Finland, for example, accepts only 13 percent of applicants and requires them to complete a two-year master's program. In Singapore, teacher training applicants are drawn from the top one-third of classes.

These educationally advanced countries are able to attract candidates to teaching and can be selective in admitting them to teacher preparation and demand longer training in part because they pay excellent salaries to their teachers. Working conditions in the schools are made attractive by collaborative planning of instruction and assessment, monitoring, demonstration lessons, and in-service training.

America's state and local school systems and our schools of education could undertake a program of curricular and teaching improvement like those we see in other nations. Certainly, such a program would have to consider the factors cited above that inhibit American students' achievement, and compensate for those conditions as much as possible. Such a program would be expensive; the rewards for students, teachers, and ultimately the entire country would amply justify the expenditures.

Nevertheless, we know that curricula and teaching methods in the U.S. can now be reformed in ways that lead to greatly improved student learning. We know these changes are possible, because they are now realities in some schools around the country. How these successful schools have reinvented themselves, and how other schools can imitate their success are the subject of part II of this book.

If we fail to improve our curriculum content and teaching strategies, it is predictable that U.S. students' average achievement will continue to decline in relation to their peers in other countries. In this technological century, a decline in our educational standards means that our nation's overall quality of life, our productivity, and prosperity will also lag behind that of other nations.

But before we sound the death knell for America's ability to produce the scientists and engineers a technologically oriented society demands, we should be mindful that our failure to meet the needs of the majority of U.S. students doesn't extend to *all* our students. A sizable number of American students, perhaps 25 percent, are being well educated and are competitive with their peers in other countries. That one-quarter of our student population is probably more than sufficient to fill the top-level positions in science and higher education, as well as in government and business.

But the dichotomy within the U.S. in educational opportunities and achievement between the relatively few "haves" and the far more numerous "have-nots" has a severe social and economic impact on those students whose schooling is mediocre or grossly inadequate, that is, those not in the top one-quarter of schools and achievement.

Those students who possess the knowledge and skills a global economy most prizes will prosper. Those who lack those qualities are limited to low-status, low-paying jobs. They do not possess the language and math background needed to function well in "second tier" jobs—positions that are not at the cutting edge of science or the highest levels of business or industry, but that must be filled by trained and competent people if our society and economy are to function. These unfortunate young people's lack of the knowledge and thinking skills also affects their ability to participate intelligently in civic life, making them easily manipulated by political demagogues or commercial hucksters.

Given the resources the U.S. possesses and expends on K–12 schooling, we should expect and could achieve substantially better results. It is the thesis of this book that adjusting schools' curricula to the specific learning needs of our varied student populations would go a long way toward reaching parity with other countries' achievement levels.

National Assessments

The United States has one assessment program that yields information on student achievement in three grades across the 50 states. Additionally, individual states administer tests to students within their borders; those measures are designed and administered by each state, based on the state's standards and curricula. Comparison of results among states can be drawn by relating scores on the states' tests with those on the national examination.

National Assessment of Educational Progress (NAEP)

First administered in 1969, NAEP reports the academic achievement of a sampling of students in grades four, eight, and twelve for all 50 states. The program is administered by the National Council for Educational Statistics (NCES) for the U.S. Department of Education. NAEP reports allow comparisons within as well as across states. Furthermore, results from certain large city districts have been available since 2002.

NAEP assesses reading, math, science, and writing at both state and national levels, and U.S. history, civics, geography, economics, world history, foreign languages, and the arts at the national level.

NAEP's scores enable each state to compare its students' achievement with that of students in other states, and to use the NAEP data as a benchmark in reviewing results of its own assessments. NAEP results and those from some states' testing programs show only modest variations, but in many states, the variations are substantial. When that is the case, the states' own assessments invariably deem far more of their students proficient than do the NAEP results.

These discrepancies speak to the lack of a common curriculum and set of standards across the 50 states. They also indicate that a wide range of difficulty levels exists among the state assessments. NAEP results are reported by percentile rank and scaled scores, but the best known NAEP metric is three achievement levels: Basic, Proficient, and Advanced. Standards for these levels are determined by a 26-member National Assessment Governing Board appointed by the Secretary for Education.

NAEP's board members are governors, state legislators, local and state officials, educators including three classroom teachers and two principals, specialists in mental measurement, business representatives, and members of the general public.

In NAEP's 2007 assessment of reading, 33 percent of fourth graders were rated Proficient. The good news is that, at grade four, the average reading score was higher than in all previous assessment years of NAEP administration. However, the percentage of high school students reading at or above proficient level declined from 40 to 35 percent. Over a five-year period, from 2002 to 2007, NAEP results for reading showed no state improved its scores, 31 were unchanged, and 12 declined.

According to ACT admissions tests results, only 50 percent of college freshmen met the colleges' benchmark for reading, that is, the ability to handle first-year reading requirements. This unhappy statistic tends to confirm the opinion of those who argue that, of all levels of schooling in the U.S., it is the high schools that most need improvement (National Assessment of Educational Progress, 2007).

State Assessments

Some states have a long history of administering their own assessments to their K–12 populations to determine the extent student learning conforms to the states' standards. The No Child Left Behind Act gave a powerful stimulus to state assessments, and they have become high stakes programs. That is, classes, teachers, and entire schools are judged and often ranked on the basis of students' performance on these exams, with penalties attached to poor performance.

Here, we will look briefly at several examples of states' assessment programs and what they tell us about state standards and curricula.

With six million students, California has a larger and far more diverse student population than many countries. Forty-eight percent of all California students were eligible for free or reduced-fee lunch. In 2007, 24.9 percent of the state's students were in English as a Second Language (ESL) classes. Note that the common terminology in popular journals is English Language Learners (ELL). Presumably, we all fall into that category; another term sometimes used is Limited English Proficient (LEP). We prefer the more descriptive term, English as Second Language.

NAEP results for California fourth graders in reading showed 21 percent as Proficient. The state's own test of fourth grade reading reported that 39 percent were Proficient.

Missouri enrolls only two percent of its student population in ESL classes, and provides free or reduced lunch to 39.1 percent. According to NAEP reports, 32 percent of Missouri's fourth graders were Proficient in reading. Missouri's state testing program reports a 34 percent proficiency rate in reading, a rare example of virtual agreement between NAEP and state test results.

In 2007, Virginia enrolled six percent of its student population in ESL courses; 31 percent received free or reduced lunches. According to NAEP reports, 38 percent of Virginia's students were Proficient in fourth grade reading while the state's own tests show 81 percent meet that criterion.

Results of state-sponsored tests in South Carolina, Massachusetts, and Missouri were most nearly consistent with NAEP scores for those states. Other states, notably Tennessee, Georgia, and Oklahoma, reported results that varied widely from NAEP results in those states. A state-by-state comparison of NAEP and state test scores can be found in *Education Next*, Spring, 2009 (Finn and Meier, 2009).

What does this sample of states tell us about students, curriculum, and assessment in the United States?

- In our most populous state, California, 25 percent of K–12 students do not speak English as their native language, and about half can be termed "poor" based on their eligibility for the subsidized school lunch program. These are staggering handicaps that few other states or countries face.
- Only one in five of California's fourth graders is a proficient reader by NAEP standards. Keep in mind that Proficient is not Advanced, the highest of three NAEP ratings.
- The rate of poverty in the three states cited suggests the need for preschool programs in language acquisition and socialization, as well as extensive diagnostic and referral programs for students with physical needs. Because some of those needs relate to diet and nutrition, schools in areas of severe poverty should provide breakfast as well as a lunch program.

- A uniform national curriculum would partially alleviate the handicap these children suffer from being frequently transferred from school to school.
- Children from impoverished families can benefit from extended school days that offer opportunities for and assistance in studying that may be lacking in their homes.
- Numerous studies have shown the relation between a community's income level and the academic achievement of students in that community (see, for example, Greene and Winters, 2006).
- Educational levels within families: students whose parents have college degrees and/or graduate and professional education will usually show higher academic achievement than those from less well-educated families.
- Expectations: both affluence and educational levels influence the expectations parents have for their children. The assumption that their children will study and learn is communicated within families and to the administrators and teachers in the schools. These parents also teach and enforce at least some standards of emotional control and social behavior for their children, and support schools' efforts to maintain those norms.
- Resources: money is important, but the most important resources for a school are supportive parents and its teachers. When administrators and trustees provide leadership and other resources, the ingredients for successful schooling are in place.

SUMMARY

- In size and other characteristics, the U.S. student population differs greatly from those of other countries.
- Among the variations, the wide range of social and economic resources in the U.S. are especially significant compared with the relative homogeneity within other nations.
- Still, the three to four decade decline in U.S. students' achievement in relation to other countries' students is a troubling sign. This widening gap does not bode well for the economic prosperity of the average American in years to come.
- Results from the Unites States' National Assessment of Educational Progress confirm that a large percentage of U.S. students are not proficient in reading, writing, and mathematics.
- Each state can select its instructional standards and the assessments that measure achievement of those standards. In many states, lax or vague standards and inadequate assessments mask the deficiencies in student learning.

Chapter 3

Replicating Success

In chapters four through seven we cite examples and present details about schools whose students show sizable gains in academic achievement. Some of these schools are in high-poverty areas with student populations that, typically, lag far behind the U.S. average in academic achievement. Other examples are drawn from privileged schools in which students are well prepared to learn and are taught in ways that result in high levels of academic achievement. A third group consists of the many schools and students who fall between the highest and lowest quartiles in achievement; call them the middle half. We cite examples of such schools that are more average in student achievement, but that show steady progress in improving learning.

Why don't more schools with similar populations and problems examine these success stories and apply similar methods to their own schools?

MAKING GOOD MATCHES: THE VARIABLES

When administrators are presented with information about high-achieving schools, they want more information about the students, faculty, and administrators, the extent of monetary and personnel support these successful schools enjoy, the attitudes of parents and the community, and so on. An administrator may then say, "I'm glad to hear of School X's success, but my community, my families and students aren't like those in School X. What works there wouldn't work in my school."

That judgment may sound like an excuse for inertia, and perhaps occasionally it is. But significant differences do exist in student populations and resources among schools; some of these variations are real impediments to students' academic achievement and resist easy change. Let's consider these factors and try to gauge the extent to which they inhibit transferring success-ful curricula from one school to another.

The most important variables are students' needs, and the curriculum content and methodologies that must be matched with those needs. This writer has been a trustee of a public (charter) school in Princeton, New Jersey. Consistently, and at every grade level, the school far outperforms state assess-ment standards as well as more demanding suburban and independent school norms. The same holds for Princeton's community school system, which also leads all but a few New Jersey schools in achievement.

Why do the great majority of students in Princeton and similar school systems succeed academically? Because their students enter school prepared to learn, their communities supply the requisite resources, and their schools provide curricula and services that correspond with the achievement levels and needs of students in these communities.

What are the characteristics of this and similarly fortunate communities, the variables that most affect students and schools?

- Affluence: educational researchers have repeatedly shown the positive rela-tion between a community's income level and the achievement of students in that community (Greene and Winters, 2006).
- Educational levels within families: students whose parents have college degrees and/or graduate and professional education will show higher academic achievement than those from less well-educated families.
- Expectations: both affluence and strong parental educational levels heighten the expectations parents hold for their children. They assume that their children will study and learn and they communicate those expecta-tions, not only to their children, but also to the administrators and teachers in their local schools. These parents also teach and enforce at least some standards of emotional control and social behavior for their children, and support the efforts of their schools to maintain those norms.
- Resources: money is important, but the most important resources for a school are its teachers and supportive parents. Schools in which students are reasonably well-behaved and eager to learn attract good teachers. When administrators and trustees provide them with leadership and support, teachers are encouraged to enter and remain in such schools.

These four elements largely explain the high level of student achievement in privileged communities. The income level in Princeton is well above the national average. The presence of a world-class university and several major research corporations guarantees a steady flow of highly educated professionals into the community.

Parents with strong educational credentials tend to make it clear to their children and local school faculties that they expect their children to do well in school; they also contribute to that end by supporting robust academic programs as well as encouraging and assisting their children to succeed in them. Teachers in such fortunate communities are under close scrutiny by parents and administrators, and most parents do not hesitate to share with administrators and school board members their opinions of the teaching their children receive. But the majority of such parents and community leaders also give credit and support to school professionals for the high quality of schooling their children enjoy. The quality of course content, the basic learning habits their pupils have largely mastered, plus adequate and enforced standards of student behavior make these schools attractive places to teach.

The abundance of resources in such communities is most obvious in the expertise they can call on in finance, organization and management, personnel administration, public relations, building construction and maintenance, and political influence. Note that if administrators or school trustees make major decisions without consulting these community resources, they run the danger of seeing letters in the local newspaper or hearing forceful criticism at the next school board meeting about deficiencies in the decision-making process.

In these privileged communities, monetary resources for teachers' salaries and physical facilities are substantial, although per pupil expenditures in these suburban systems are sometimes lower than in less successful inner-city schools.

WHAT WORKS IN PRIVILEGED COMMUNITIES?

Given these abundant resources, what curricula have communities with high-achieving schools put in place?

First, these schools try to match the demands of course work with the achievement level of their students.

Even schools with very high average test scores have some students whose achievement lags. Those whose progress is far below state or local norms are conspicuous in schools with a high-achieving population. In well-run schools, those students who are falling behind are identified by their teachers, who discuss possible in-school remedial steps, for example, regular tutoring.

Teachers also meet with the students' parents to explain their schools' efforts, pledge frequent updates on classroom performance, and ask for greater participation of parents in supervising students' study time at home. Of course, if these steps are important in high-achieving districts, they are absolutely essential in chronically low-achieving schools.

Second, for students at the upper end of academic achievement, curricula in successful schools include rigorous courses that challenge even the highest achieving students. Virtually all such high schools offer a broad array of Advanced Placement and/or International Baccalaureate courses that enable students to undertake college-level work in high school.

Third, a high level of student achievement and community resources make possible interesting and complex projects that permit able students to work cooperatively in applying their "book knowledge." Such schools also have ready access to museums, research laboratories, and historical sites; they frequently can arrange partnerships with local colleges' programs for credit courses or enrichment activities.

Traditional educators tend to be suspicious of "projects." When such activities substitute for instruction that requires systematic study for knowledge and information, that suspicion is well-founded, although progressive educators might disagree. But even conservative educators would concede that projects that complement the school curriculum, enrich students' cultural knowledge, and simply offer an occasional break from the daily routine of school are valuable experiences for students.

The following chapters will exemplify how high-achieving schools work. Here, let's simply note that successful school systems offer a range of curricula that respond to the needs of their students, from those struggling with basic knowledge and skills to those who learn at very advanced levels.

WHAT WORKS IN DISADVANTAGED COMMUNITIES?

Some ten miles from Princeton in New Jersey's capital, Trenton, public schools score abysmally low on the state assessments. Why don't Trenton schools imitate the practices that are successful in neighboring Princeton? Because the characteristics of high-achieving suburban schools—affluence, high community education levels, parental and teachers' expectations for student behavior and achievement, and resources—are largely lacking in Trenton and similar inner-city schools.

There is no question that these deficiencies make the efforts of urban schools to provide an adequate education far more difficult. Nor can reinvigorating the schools in our major cities be possible without strong, sustained leadership that gains the cooperation of parents, teachers, and students.

Nevertheless, schools now exist at every level and in all parts of the country that have, to a significant extent, overcome the educational handicaps imposed by severe poverty; the majority of their students are succeeding academically.

The changes these successful schools make begin by their asking, "What content and teaching methods match our students' needs?" Having identified curricula that correspond to their students' current achievement levels, school staff then rally the support of parents and the students themselves for the behavioral norms and instructional practices that these students need.

These changes require careful planning on the part of teachers, administrators, and trustees, an ability and commitment on the part of teachers to adapt their subject matter and teaching strategies to their students, and an ongoing information program for parents, with firm insistence on their cooperation. In other words, these failing inner-city schools must imitate their more privileged and successful suburban counterparts in gearing their curricula and behavioral norms to the learning status and needs of their students.

The needs of our most disadvantaged children differ from and are more challenging than those in students in suburban schools. Only by adapting the curriculum and enforcing behavioral standards in ways that respond to the realities of inner-city students' lives can schools that serve our most economically and educationally impoverished students succeed.

Would such changes in our lowest achieving schools enable their students to equal the achievement of students in more affluent schools? That is possible; some schools that serve severely disadvantaged populations like North Star Academy or Robert Treat Charter School, both in Newark, outperform almost every other school in New Jersey. Chapters four through seven describe other schools that have overcome the challenges of severe poverty and language. Their students are achieving at a rate equal to and sometimes surpassing that of their suburban counterparts.

But students and schools in our most disadvantaged communities face problems in their daily lives that impinge not only on academic achievement, but on their physical, emotional, and social development. Successful schools can facilitate the learning that inspires hope in those who suffer from the problems that rack our worst neighborhoods and inhibit young people's development. Gangs, street violence, absence of male models, lack of meaningful jobs, inadequate access to medical care, and other realities in the lives of many inner-city youngsters all take a toll on students' lives

Good schools can provide the fundamental knowledge and skills students need to stay in and progress in school, along with behavioral standards that equip them to function in a workplace or the general society. With this help from their schools many, but not all students will overcome some, but not all of the problems of their environment. That's less than what we desire for all children, but vastly better than current general failure of schools attended by our most disadvantaged students.

SUCCESSFUL STUDENTS: PRINCIPLES AND PRACTICES

Families, teachers, and administrators all play important roles in successful schools. Again, we refer readers to chapters four through seven for examples and specific activities.

In Families

The knowledge and attitudes that contribute to student learning begin long before a child enters school and continue throughout his schooling. These important contributions begin by instilling the social and emotional controls that enable students and their classmates to learn.

The family's second major contribution comes from furthering their children's language development in preschool years; such learning comes informally through frequent oral exchanges, as well as from parents or older siblings reading to younger children. When children hear adults speak supportively of their teachers and their school's rules for study, homework, and extra-school projects, they are given an important message—even if they don't always agree.

In Classrooms

The chief task of schools, especially elementary schools, is to equip their young charges with the basic knowledge and skills they need in order to progress in later schooling and throughout their lives. In the primary grades, teaching should focus mainly on language acquisition and use: reading, writing, speaking, and listening. The second basic is learning mathematics; for children in primary grades, this instruction should emphasize embedding in their memories basic math information they need to call on in later math studies, for example, the multiplication tables.

A base of general knowledge supports learning and, to a great extent, is a prerequisite for it. Children whose parents can take the time to speak with and read to them on a range of daily topics are providing the context that enables young students to make sense of what they are taught in school. But some children don't enjoy that advantage. Primary grade teachers can help to reduce the deficit by reading to their classes and giving students books they can read in and out of school.

The Role of Administrators

All school administrators and teachers want their students to learn. When significant numbers of their students are failing, true to human nature, teachers and administrators are inclined to blame the students' out-of-school environment, which can, in fact, be an enormous hindrance to academic achievement. Since school officials can do little to change those circumstances, they are in danger of becoming apathetic, feeling defeated by forces beyond their control.

Chapters four through seven cite examples of schools that have substantially, if not completely, created an environment in which seriously disadvantaged students do learn. To achieve such success, administrators, working with their teachers, must be willing to reconsider the content of the curriculum and, especially, the methods of delivering that content in the classroom. And they must commit themselves, with input from parents and students, to generating and enforcing a set of rules for study and appropriate behavior.

Administrators who analyze their student's needs, then undertake the in-service instruction and practices that instituting alternative curricula requires' can considerably, sometimes dramatically improve the achievement levels of their students. That enhanced academic success in turn can change students' lives, giving them hope for success in school and beyond.

SUMMARY

Successful schools determine the specific learning needs of their students, then they select the curriculum content and methodologies that respond most effectively to those needs. The requirement that any curriculum innovation must be tailored to the particular needs of a student population means that for a school to replicate another school's successful program the two schools should have roughly similar challenges and resources.

The variables that most affect student learning are:

• The level of affluence within a community
• The level of education within families
• Parents' and teachers' expectations for students' academic achievement
• Resources, especially the quality of the teaching staff.

Schools can be most successful when they have forged close cooperation between families, teachers, as well as local and district administrators.

Part II

Solutions

In the chapters that follow on successful elementary, middle, and high schools, we focus on three factors in each school:

- *Demography* refers to the principal characteristics of a school, its community, and its student population. Teachers and administrators can find schools that resemble theirs and have been successful in raising student achievement.
- *Achievement* offers the evidence that the listed schools have, in fact, succeeded in improving students' academic achievement. The measure most frequently cited is scores on state-mandated assessments, but other indicators like graduation rates, college admissions, and awards will be cited.
- *Interventions* describe the programs that these successful schools have introduced and that seem to have contributed significantly to student achievement.

We will examine schools that vary widely in terms of their students' readiness to learn and the resources available to the community and the schools. What they have in common is that their students *are* learning: they have shown substantial improvement in students' academic success, the lowest achieving as well as the highest achieving schools, and those in between.

Virtually every teacher and administrator can find one or more schools that look very much like theirs in these descriptions of successful schools. The match won't be perfect; there are too many variables that contribute to student achievement to achieve identical matches. But comparisons can be made on the basis of common elements that most affect student achievement.

By "elementary schools," we refer to those that have pre-kindergarten through grade five; some districts include grade five in middle school. Middle school means grades four or five through grade eight. High school incorporates grades nine through twelve.

One might contend that all grades are equally important, but we argue that the introductory years of schooling are "more equal" in importance than others. In elementary school the basic tools for virtually all future academic learning are taught. When they are learned well, students are launched on a path to success in their middle and high school years. Conversely, educational research has repeatedly shown that students whose knowledge and skills in language and math are seriously deficient by third to fourth grade can only be salvaged by large-scale and persistent efforts to remediate the deficiencies. In many of our poorest schools, that recovery is not realized, and failing third graders become failing middle schoolers, who become high school dropouts.

In holding to our intent to speak primarily to the content and methods of the academic curriculum, we won't say much about how schools cope with the need to inculcate at least minimal social and emotional behavior in their young charges. We note, however, that a host of consultants and publications offer their prescriptions for achieving that goal. Some useful resources are: *The Social Skills Curriculum Library*, by Ruth Weltman Begun (1995), and Kathy Beland's article on improving social and emotional competence (2007).

In chapter four, we will consider elementary schools with seriously disadvantaged students that have notably raised their students' achievement. Chapters five and six cover the same ground for middle and high schools. In each chapter we also will examine schools that have a history of success, but haven't coasted on their reputations and continue to improve. And we'll examine the category of schools that are at neither extreme of resources and achievement; we'll see how some of them have introduced programs that have brought about steady improvement.

When we speak of *disadvantaged*, *more average*, or *notably advantaged* schools and students, we refer to the demographic factors that typically correlate with school success. These factors largely group themselves under the general categories of *affluence* or *poverty* in the community and families that a school serves. Among the principal indicators are:

• Community and local school population income levels,
• Percentage of students on free or reduced lunch program,
• Parents' educational background,
• Percentage of students who are non-native English speakers.

Note that these factors *correlate* with school achievement; that relationship is demonstrable. The extent to which they *cause* success or failure is far more difficult to establish. At any rate, the problematic factors are, to a large extent, beyond the control of schools. But successful schools recognize their impact on student achievement, adjust their teaching, and supply some services that can ameliorate these handicaps to student achievement.

An encouraging discovery in this author's investigation is the existence of many successful schools and school systems. The schools profiled in succeeding chapters are selected from various areas of the country and community environments. Ours is only a sample; many more examples could be cited of faculty and administrators successfully teaching their students, whatever the demographic factors of their communities.

Chapter 4

Elementary Schools

INTRODUCTION

This book primarily addresses preparation for and instruction in academic learning. As noted in part I, the physical, social, and emotional preparation of children for school is arguably as important as their intellectual development. Those who enter school with underdeveloped knowledge and skills in language can be moved forward with intensive efforts by a school. But children who begin the early years of school in poor health, or without having mastered minimal social skills and emotional controls pose a more difficult problem; it's one that teachers and administrators must work to remedy, as much as possible with parents, if these disadvantaged youngsters and their classmates are to learn.

Because our primary focus is academic achievement, we won't attempt to describe how schools cope with the need to inculcate appropriate social and emotional behavior in their young charges. For more information on this important topic, see the publications mentioned in the introduction to part II, p. 30.

In this chapter we profile three kinds of elementary schools: one type is schools with a majority of seriously disadvantaged students that have notably raised their students' achievement. We will also examine several schools that are at neither extreme of resources and the preparation of their incoming students; we'll see how some of these average schools have introduced programs that resulted in steady gains in student learning. Thirdly, we will look at highly successful schools whose students live in advantaged communities and who enter school well prepared to learn; the schools we cite haven't become complacent; they continue to improve and their students continue to grow.

To say that these factors typically correlate with school achievement is not to say that they *cause* achievement or the lack of it. These qualities create conditions that are typically associated with student learning. Nevertheless, non-achievers exist in some affluent, resource-rich schools, as do some outstanding learners among students in poverty or those who have serious deficiencies in their English language skills.

We look first at those elementary schools, most of whose students enter school with substantial disadvantages and deficiencies in academic learning. The most conspicuous problem these four- to six-year-olds suffer from is a lack of the knowledge and skills related to language acquisition. Because that knowledge and those skills are so critical for all future learning, we'll mention practices, principally within their families, that can provide strong academic preparation for children's earliest years of schooling, and the consequences of that preparation, or the lack of it. We will then show profiles of three schools whose high-achieving students are drawn from communities with substantial social and economic advantages.

Parents contribute to language development in their young children by:

• Talking with them and reading to them from their earliest years
• Listening and asking them to expand or explain their comments
• Playing word games
• Encouraging them to ask questions.

These practices are common in affluent families and are relatively absent in families in severe poverty. Two researchers (Hart and Risley, 2003) put numbers on the enormous variations between early language experiences of children from families headed by professionals versus those from welfare families. By age three, the children of professionals had heard an average of over eight million more words than children from welfare families. The professionals' children had spoken over four million more words than the welfare children. The oral vocabulary of the professional family children exceeded not only the children but that of the parents of the welfare families.

In the Hart and Risley studies, parenting measures accounted for 59 percent of a three-year-old's cognitive accomplishment (IQ measure). In a follow-up study of the same children, aged nine and ten, early parenting measures accounted for 61 percent of variance in measures of cognitive ability. So the gap in language skills remained and even increased slightly after several years of school.

Several of the schools described below receive a majority of their students from drastically poor families. Their teachers in the earliest grades face many of the problems suggested by the grim figures of the Hart and Risley studies just mentioned. Through carefully planned and monitored efforts, these schools are succeeding in overcoming much of their students' language deficit, enabling many children to move into middle school with adequate knowledge and skills in reading, listening, speaking, and writing.

Three further points: poverty, like affluence, is a relative term. In describing schools that work successfully with poor children, this text relies primarily on a school population's enrollment in the free or reduced lunch program, a commonly used definition of poverty, but a very general one. Not all children in a lunch program come from severely impoverished families. And certainly not all parents in impoverished homes fail to communicate in ways that aid their children's language skills, but a significant percentage do.

A second note relates to the communication deficit experienced by children for whom English is a second language, and who live in families in which English is not the language used in the home. Certainly, some children arrive in pre-kindergarten fluent in both English and another language native to them and their parents, but these fortunate young learners are very much the exception. The great majority of English as a Second Language learners have modest English communication skills. Because a disproportionate number of their families are poor, the children also suffer from other handicaps to early learning.

Third, young children whose language skills are minimal are sometimes categorized as incapable of learning at satisfactory or advanced levels. In fact, when these children have benefitted from vigorous language remediation programs, their IQ scores often soar dramatically. These youngsters are not candidates for special education classes: they simply need words, grammar, basic contextual knowledge, and the other language skills that enable them to learn and communicate.

Let's examine some elementary schools that have shown strong results in lifting the achievement levels of children: those who arrive poorly prepared to learn, and others in more advantaged communities.

TEN SUCCESSFUL ELEMENTARY SCHOOLS

Garfield Elementary School, Long Beach, California

Garfield is a K–5 school in Long Beach, California. In 2003, the Long Beach Unified School District received the Broad Prize for urban school districts that show great progress in improving the academic achievement of their disadvantaged students.

The school's enrollment is about 1,000 students. Some 93 percent of Garfield's student body receives free or subsidized lunch, a very high percentage even in a state with many impoverished students. The 60 percent of Garfield students for whom English is a second language represent a number that is double the average for California, a state with one of the highest proportion of ESL students. Long Beach is called "One of the most diverse cities in the U.S.," a distinction that often, as here, means a very high proportion of immigrants.

Despite its considerable disadvantages, Garfield ranks among the top 10th percentile of like schools in California; in third grade language arts, for example, Garfield students surpassed the achievement levels of the top 10 comparable schools. Over a five-year period, Garfield students at all grade levels and for all subgroups have exceeded the state growth targets set for them.

How do they do it? What programs and interventions have enabled Garfield to achieve so admirable a record?

A general principle repeatedly mentioned by the school's faculty is, "Excellence and failure, both in academic achievement and social behavior, are recognized *immediately* at Garfield." This practice of promptly applauding students for their positive accomplishments and swiftly intervening when achievement or behavior does not meet expectations is a common theme in successful elementary schools.

By far the greatest emphasis at Garfield is on teaching the knowledge and skills required in reading, writing, and mathematics. A constant at Garfield is the use of Direct Instruction, both for inculcating fundamental skills and for teaching higher level thinking. This teaching methodology is fast-paced, structured, and teacher-directed, with questions constantly posed to students to hold their attention and assess what they have learned. The basic reading texts are the Open Court series. These readers and assessment materials are mandated by the Long Beach District; they have a strong, but not exclusive emphasis on phonics and the basic mechanics of early reading instruction.

District and local school leaders ensure that teachers implement the standards-aligned curriculum and use the Pacing Guide the school district requires to keep lessons on schedule within each class and among classes at the same grade level. All fourth and fifth grades have reduced class size three times a week to permit specialists to provide direct instruction in writing.

All Garfield students participate in California's Home Reading Club, which requires nightly reading.

After-school tutoring is provided for those falling behind in their classes. Project Excel offers special programs for accelerated learners.

The Garfield Academy of Professional Development offers extensive opportunities for teacher learning. This program provides teachers with substantial time and funding for large- and small-group learning activities.

On Grade-Level Release days, teachers meet in grade-level teams to assess student reports and other data on student achievement, and to plan their classroom interventions.

Ida Burns Elementary School, Conway, Arkansas

This school in the Conway, Arkansas, School District has a student population that is, on average, moderately but not severely disadvantaged. Some 43 percent of Ida Burns students receive free or reduced-fee lunches. Only two percent are classified as ESL students, and 15 percent of the students receive special education.

The school's results on the state assessments show solid advantages over the state averages, with 82 percent of Ida Burns students scoring at proficiency level versus the state average of 69 percent (2004). In the mathematics portion of the state tests, 79 percent of Ida Burns students were proficient, compared with 65 percent at the state level.

Among the array of interventions the district, principals, and teachers have implemented to advance their students' academic performance are:

- Each grade level has timelines with defined expectations for instruction; these points are aligned with the Arkansas state standards.
- All classes strongly emphasize language learning. As one Ida Burns teacher said, "Language is not a subject, it is the means by which all other subjects are pursued."
- Each class at Ida Burns has a "buddy class," in which primary and intermediate classes are paired. Students meet weekly to read, write, and work together.
- The faculty has nine and a half days per year of professional development. All teachers meet monthly in grade-level sessions to ensure coordination of content and schedules.

Webster Elementary School, Syracuse, New York

This school of 560 students is part of the Syracuse, New York, School district. About 80 percent of the students receive free or reduced-fee lunches, a figure that is almost double the state average. The school reports no students designated "limited English proficiency."

In the 2004 state assessments, 62 percent of grade four Webster students met or exceeded state standards in language arts. This figure compares with the school district's 39 percent, and the state-wide average of 63 percent. In mathematics, 97 percent of Webster's grade four students met or exceeded state proficiency standards, compared with a 63 percent average for the school district, and 79 percent at the state level.

Webster's teachers say that "Reading is most important, the number one subject." Every day Webster students have a two-hour block of time devoted to language arts.

The district-wide curriculum, based on state standards, specifies outcomes for each grade level. The curriculum includes vocabulary listings and samples of grades four and eight English language assessments from the state examinations, with scoring rubrics and timelines for assessments.

Webster's teachers credit much of the school's success to strong leadership on the part of their principal, who supports them and involves them in decisions. The development of the district's teacher evaluation and improvement plan, a frequent cause of controversy in school districts, has been cited as a model of cooperation between the district and the teachers' union.

Teachers at Webster recognize that their obligations to their students extend beyond academic learning; they try to deal with the problems that many of their students bring to school. Teachers say, "For two-thirds of our kids, this [school] is the best part of their day. This is home for them."

Beard Elementary School, Northside School District, San Antonio, Texas

Beard enrolls some 1,090 students in pre-kindergarten through grade five. The median household income for the district is $42,900 compared with the Texas median of $46,900 and $49,200 for the U.S. The percentage of Beard students eligible for free/reduced-fee lunch is seven percent; the figure for Texas is 56 percent. Just two percent of Beard students participate in an English as Second Language program, compared with a state average of 16 percent. One half of enrolled students are White, 35 percent Hispanic, eight percent are Asian, and five percent African-American. In terms of demographic indicators, Beard students and their families appear to fall somewhere in the "middle half," between economically disadvantaged and affluent.

On the Great Schools Ratings, Beard receives the top rank of 10, and Beard parents give the school the highest rating of five stars.

The Texas Education Agency awarded the school a "Commended Performance" in reading/English language arts, mathematics, science, and writing. The school was rated "Exemplary" in 2008 by the Texas Education Agency, and received a Gold Performance award.

On the Texas Assessment of Knowledge and Skills (TAKS) in 2008, 100 percent of Beard's grade five students met or exceeded standards, versus the state average of 83 percent. In science, 98 percent of Beard's students met or exceeded standards, compared with 81 percent across the state. Ninety-nine percent of Beard's fifth graders met or exceeded the mathematics standards as opposed to 83 percent statewide.

An interesting feature of Beard's curriculum is the wide range of games and other activities the school uses to reinforce the basic curriculum and texts. For example, a Consonant Blend Scavenger Hunt for first graders; fifth graders engage in Playground Physics and the Mean, Median, and Mode Card Game. Not all activities are so directly related to curricular knowledge and skills, but they offer welcome breaks from classroom routine while complementing academic instruction.

Robert Treat Academy, Newark, New Jersey

This New Jersey charter school enrolls 450 students in grades K–12. The median household income for the school's zip code is $28,260, versus the state figure of $55,510.

Newark is New Jersey's largest city. A number of major corporations have headquarters there, but generally, the city is marked by severe poverty. The area attracts many immigrants, especially from Spanish-speaking countries. The Newark public schools have a long record of unsatisfactory performance, leading some ten years ago to a state takeover of the system. In the last two to three years, the school system has made improvements and some state controls have been relaxed. The failures of the school system have prompted many Newark parents to apply to the charter schools that have flourished in that city. One of these is the Robert Treat Academy.

In the 2007 state assessment in language arts, 77.9 percent of Treat Academy students rated "proficient," and an additional 18.6 were classified as "advanced proficient." In mathematics, 43.4 percent were "proficient," and a remarkable 55.2 percent rated "advanced proficient." The cumulative proficiency scores of 96.5 percent in language arts and 98.6 percent in mathematics give Treat Academy the highest ranking among New Jersey public schools.

In 2008, Robert Treat Academy was named a national Blue Ribbon School, and a Title I School of Distinction. The school's outstanding record of achievement has attracted substantial funding from non-public sources, both local corporations and national foundations.

Like many inner-city charter schools, Treat Academy has lengthened its instructional day, and holds classes 11 months of the year. Despite this heavy schedule, the school's average daily attendance is 96.6 percent.

The school's homework policy urges parents to create conditions in the home that permit students to complete their homework. The policy statement also says,

"Let your child take full responsibility for doing his/her homework and getting it to school on time, including accepting the consequences of not getting it to school on time." The school has both homework detention for those who must accept the consequences of non-compliance, and a homework help center.

The Academy pours considerable effort into a High School Placement Department. The school's goal is to give as many parents as possible options for where their children will attend high school. The Placement Department has helped to send Treat graduates to many elite independent schools on the East Coast, as well as public and private schools that are less prestigious, but still allow them to bypass the Newark school system's high schools.

Treat Academy has outstanding facilities, thanks to grants and external funding sources. The building is state of the art, with technology and science laboratories, a media center, and a fine arts and music pavilion.

Classes at Treat have more students than is typical of elementary schools, averaging about 25 students per class. However, every classroom has a certified teacher plus an assistant, who may also be certified. This practice of having two adults in a classroom appears increasingly common, and offers many advantages in terms of individualizing instruction, overseeing students' work, and managing student behavior. It also moderates the classroom isolation that many teachers find troublesome. Increasing the number of teachers is, of course, expensive, although increasing the number of students in a class can give some budgetary relief.

Cuyahoga Heights Elementary School, Cuyahoga, Ohio

This school of some 350 students includes grades pre-K–5. Cuyahoga Heights is five miles from the center of downtown Cleveland. Median household income for the district is $45,200; the Ohio median is $47,500, and the U.S. figure is $49,200. These figures suggest a school population that is neither severely disadvantaged nor highly affluent.

In the school year 2007–08, the school met all 30 of the state's indicators of quality. On Ohio's statewide assessment program, 88.3 percent of grade five students at Cuyahoga Heights were adjudged proficient or above; the Ohio figure was 72.7 percent. In mathematics, 80 percent of the school's students were proficient, versus 61.8 percent statewide. Assessment scores fluctuated noticeably in grade five; the previous year (2006–07), Cuyahoga Heights students averaged 94.5 percent in both reading and math. Students in grades three and four of this school showed consistent upward progress in both reading and math.

In 2008, Cuyahoga Heights Elementary School received the Blue Ribbon Lighthouse School Award. In the same year, the school was recognized as

"Outstanding" by the Harvard Business Club. In 1998, the Ohio Association of Elementary School Principals named the school a "Hall of Fame School." In the Great Schools rating, Cuyahoga Heights Elementary received the top score of 10.

One reason for the school's success is its extensive and systematic practices for evaluating curriculum. Every four to five years, each curriculum area conducts a self-evaluation with the assistance of a local university or the Ohio Department of Education. The self-evaluation is followed by faculty planning for curriculum revisions, then decisions about textbook adoptions; this schedule attempts to ensure that the texts selected conform to the faculty-designed curriculum.

Grades K–1, 2–3, and 4–5 are paired as teachers at Cuyahoga Heights "loop" up to the next grade with their students for one year. Besides providing for greater continuity in curriculum, this practice encourages a more familiar relationship between teachers and their young students.

Arbor Creek Elementary School, Olathe, Kansas

Arbor Creek School enrolls 660 students in grades pre-K–6. Daily attendance is 96 percent. Just 2.1 percent of Arbor Creek's students qualify for free/reduced-fee lunch versus a state average of 42.8 percent, so Arbor Creek's students certainly cannot be termed disadvantaged.

On the 2008 Kansas State Assessment, 100 percent of Arbor Creek's sixth graders were proficient in reading compared with a state average of 85 percent. In math as well, 100 percent of the school's sixth grade students were rated proficient. Arbor Creek is a Blue Ribbon Lighthouse school.

Before and after the school day teachers meet with students in small groups to give additional help in reading and math.

Beginning in kindergarten, students meet with a Computer Learning Specialist, who reinforces the role of technology in classroom learning.

The school provides extended day care for kindergarten students.

Family Learning in Partnerships (FLIP) offers day and evening sessions for families of pre-kindergarten through grade three students. In these sessions, parents hear ideas and view demonstrations of learning activities parents can implement in their homes.

Graham Road Elementary School (GRES), Falls Church, Virginia

GRES is part of the Fairfax County school system, in the Washington DC metropolitan area. The school reports that 51 percent of its students are of Limited English Proficiency, with 41 percent in ESL programs. The free/

reduced lunch program enrolls 80.5 percent of the students. The Fairfax County system reports a mobility rate for each of its schools: for GRES, that rate is 36 percent annual turnover in the student body, a factor that poses enormous problems in curriculum continuity for its students.

In 2008, GRES was named a National Blue Ribbon School.

On the Virginia Standards of Learning (SOL) assessment program (2007–08), grade three GRES students had an average pass rate in reading of 64.3 percent; in mathematics, the average was 92.3. Average scores for GRES third graders in 2006–07 were reading, 86.2, mathematics, 91.7. In the school year 2005–06 reading average was 87.1, and math pass rate was 100 percent. These year-to-year fluctuations may be attributable to relatively small numbers of students in grade three, but the high student turnover rate also makes year-to-year comparisons difficult. A substantially different student body is being measured every year.

GRES is a focus school for language and fine arts. These subjects are integrated with each other, and with courses in other academic areas. Additional time is allocated for the visual arts, and GRES has a weekly Art Integration Program for grades four and five, which art and science or social studies instructors teach jointly.

The Reading Recovery Program is an intensive effort to help first graders become independent readers and quickly reach their grade level in achievement.

The Title I reading teacher at GRES works with struggling students, but also with her colleagues to integrate good reading practices into all classes.

Capitol View Elementary School (CVES), Atlanta, Georgia

CVES is part of the Atlanta Public School System, with some 250 students in grades K–5. Eighty-eight percent of the students are in the free/reduced-fee lunch program.

In 2006, 100 percent of CVES students met state proficiency standards in reading, math, language arts, social studies, and science.

The school achieved Annual Yearly Progress (AYP) status for seven successive years. CVES is ranked in the top five percent of Georgia elementary schools.

In 2004, the school received the National Blue Ribbon Award for excellence. CVES was a finalist for the Excellence in Education awards, presented by the Center for Urban School Transformation.

The school received the Dispelling the Myth award that is presented yearly to five schools in the nation. This recognition is by the Education Trust for strong achievement in educating low-income students of color.

Since 2003, CVES has been a Core Knowledge school. This program has two components, one for preschool, used in some 300 programs nationally, and the more familiar one for grades K–8, which is found in some 770 schools. As the name suggests, Core Knowledge offers basic content, logically developed, in a sequence that avoids gaps or repetition.

The school prides itself on holding high expectations for students' academic progress, with prompt identification and remediation for struggling students. There is also a vigorous professional development program for teachers.

Snow Creek Elementary School, Penhook, Virginia

Snow Creek is a rural school with some 200 students in grades K–5. Fifty-five percent of its students are eligible for free or reduced-fee lunch.

In 2004, just 40 percent of Snow Creek's students were rated proficient in reading on Virginia's Standards of Learning (SOL) assessment, compared with the state-wide average of 71 percent. After two years of intensive intervention, the school's students surpassed state averages in every subject and at every grade level. In grade five, 96 percent of the students were proficient in reading, and 100 percent were proficient in mathematics.

Snow Creek's remarkable turn-around in student achievement was recognized by the Title I Distinguished School Award.

This great leap forward was sparked by the principal, who formed teacher teams that developed common formative assessments. In team meetings, teachers reviewed each student's progress on essential skills, and identified struggling students. The resulting interventions brought specialists and other support staff, including the principal, to join the teachers in conducting intensive instructional periods, with students grouped by their status and progress in specific skills.

SUCCESSFUL PROGRAMS IN ELEMENTARY SCHOOLS

What practices and programs seem to account for the successes in the schools profiled above?

1. High expectations for all students, frequent formative assessment, and prompt, intensive remediation for faltering students; these factors in combination appear highly correlated with student achievement. This is conspicuously true in schools with large populations of disadvantaged students.

Garfield Elementary School and Capitol View Elementary School especially illustrate how these attitudes and practices can affect students' academic performance.

2. A heavy emphasis on English language skills, particularly reading and writing. Schools with a high percentage of economically disadvantaged and/or English as Second Language students especially stress language learning. This is the case in almost all of the schools we have profiled, notably so in Ida Burns and Webster elementary schools.

3. Increased instructional hours; these include more hours in the school day, Saturday classes, and an 11-month school year. A noteworthy example of the impact of extra teaching time is seen in the Robert Treat Academy.

4. A carefully sequenced curriculum that emphasizes content knowledge characterizes several of our exemplary schools, most obviously Capitol View School with its Core Knowledge program.

5. Professional development for teachers that is planned cooperatively by teachers and administrators is a common element in most successful schools, elementary through high school. Good examples at the elementary level are Ida Burns and Garfield elementary schools.

6. In the schools we cite, teachers' schedules are organized in ways that promote cooperation in planning and coordination in curriculum. Grade-level teams coordinate instruction, and common assessments encourage individual and group diagnosis and remediation. Snow Creek Elementary School has used this organizational strategy with great success.

Chapter 5

Middle Schools

INTRODUCTION

They're sometimes called the "tweens." Between ages 10 and 14, students move from a structured, closely monitored classroom environment to one in which they are expected to take more responsibility for organizing their school work and planning their daily and longer term study schedule. Their courses are more difficult and grading is more stringent. Students who master these new demands and prove able to move from the basic knowledge and skills learned in early grades to the more complex requirements of mathematics, science, reading, and writing will succeed in middle school. And success in middle school means a readiness to undertake the greater demands of high school subjects.

At the same time, these youngsters are experiencing substantial transitions in their physical and emotional development, and their reasoning skills are becoming increasingly complex. These developments are further complicated by powerful new influences on middle schoolers' social lives as peer friendships become enormously important.

So, in middle school, teachers concentrate on:

- Professional development activities that focus on upgrading subject-matter knowledge, as well as teaching strategies and motivation enhancements that are appropriate for this age group.
- Clear rules and consistent application of behavioral norms. "Fairness" is a primary virtue for middle schoolers.
- Prompt intervention for struggling students. As the demands of course content increase, laggards must be helped to bring themselves up to speed as quickly as possible.

- Personal relations of teachers with their students change from the familial, nurturing type in primary grades to the more objective but supportive role of adult counselors.
- Staying organized becomes extremely important as students are now expected to keep track of their assignments, meet deadlines, deal with demands of various teachers, and schedule long-term assignments.

These concerns lead many educators to label their middle school students as the most challenging ones to teach. That opinion receives support from the widespread decline in academic growth in grades five through eight, as indicated in state assessments and NAEP scores. Gains from elementary school often remain stagnant or slip away; those students who were low achievers in the elementary grades begin to fall still farther behind their classmates.

As in our survey of elementary schools, this chapter examines middle schools whose student bodies vary widely. Again, our primary focus is on schools with students from seriously disadvantaged communities and families. We also profile other schools whose students are drawn from families and communities that possess greater resources.

What all of these schools have in common is high student achievement: their students surpass their peers in academic achievement. We describe some guiding policies and programs in these schools that appear to bring about superior learning. In describing these programs we use the comments of the schools' faculties, as well as those of outside observers. For more objective information, we depend heavily on results from state assessment programs that corroborate student progress.

We reiterate briefly here the demographic factors associated with academic learning that we described in chapter four. They are:

- The income level of a community and a school's population
- The educational background of parents
- The proportion of students who are non-native English speakers
- The percentage of students in free or reduced-fee lunch programs.

SEVEN SUCCESSFUL MIDDLE SCHOOLS

Von Steuben Middle School, Peoria, Illinois

This middle school has some 400 students in grades five through eight. Fifty-eight percent of the students receive free or reduced lunches, a figure well below that of the school district, but in excess of the U.S. averages. Von

Steuben has a mobility rate of 22 percent, so continuity in the curriculum is a challenge. But the school's attendance rate is a respectable 94 percent.

In grade eight, 79 percent of students met or exceeded state standards in reading (2004). The district's number was 57 percent, and that for the state was 54 percent. Sixty percent of grade eight students met or exceeded state standards in mathematics, versus the district's 47 percent and the state-wide average of 54 percent.

Von Steuben's professional development activities focus on ensuring that teachers make the connections, by grade and subject level, between state standards and the daily curriculum and lesson plans in the classrooms.

The school uses the Open Court reading series; the publisher, SRA, provided two years of a staff developer's time to coordinate training in teaching and assessing results of the reading program. In grades five and six, the results of weekly student assessments are forwarded to building and district administrators.

Struggling students are offered an extended day, in which tutors and mentors are available; the schedule also includes "homework Saturdays" and help with assignments during lunch period. Students who are lagging behind their classmates can also attend summer school and participate in a special district program: Reaching Academic Potential (RAP).

KIPP Ujima Village Academy, Baltimore, Maryland

This charter school has some 300 students in grades five through eight. Eighty-six percent of its students receive free or reduced-fee lunch. The school has no entrance requirements or selection criteria. Most entering students perform far below their academic grade level.

The KIPP Ujima Village Academy has met all state standards every year of its operation. In 2006, on the Maryland School Assessment (MSA) the school's sixth, seventh, and eighth graders achieved the highest math scores in the state, with passing rates of 100 percent. In reading, sixth graders also achieved the highest reading scores in the city, and outperformed the state average by 20 percent.

What are the qualities and interventions that contribute to this school's outstanding achievement?

- The school has a strong founding principal who enjoys considerable autonomy.
- Funding is more than adequate, with public funds supplemented by private grants.
- The school's enrollment is just 300 students, and it has small classes.
- Students have a longer than usual school day, week, and year (see basic principles below).

The school's staff and board believe the school's success is owed to five basic principles:

1. High Expectations: All students are expected to achieve and ultimately, to matriculate in college.
2. More Time on Task: At Ujima, the school day is at least 9.25 hours during the regular school year, 6.25 hours for three weeks in summer, and 3.5 hours every Saturday throughout the year.
3. Choice and Commitment: All students, parents, and staff choose to be part of the school and make a commitment to meet its expectations.
4. Power to Lead: The school has the authority for staffing, budgeting, and for teaching according to students' needs.
5. Focus on Results: "Success" depends on demonstrated student achievement and ultimately, on how many students graduate from college.

Gaspar de Portola Middle School, San Diego, California

This school in a large urban area of southern California has some 1,050 students in grades six through eight. Thirty-one percent of its students qualify for free or reduced lunches. Eight percent are in ESL classes.

In 2005, on the state's achievement index (API) the school received a score of 811, representing a gain of 36 points over the 2001–02 school year. The school met all 25 criteria for Annual Yearly Progress (AYP). In 2003, the school was named a "California Distinguished School."

Each teacher posts and adverts to a daily class agenda or essential study questions that relate to state-district standards. During the school day, teachers help students stay on track by referring to the posting.

In grade six, English classes are taught in two-hour blocks. For grades seven and eight, the school offers support classes in math and English. The school has an extended day for both math and English teaching, with tutoring targeted to specific math skills.

Westbury Middle School, Westbury, New York

This middle school is part of the Westbury Union Free School District on Long Island. The school enrolls 850 students in grades six through eight. Seventy-four percent of Westbury Middle School students are eligible for free or reduced-fee lunches. The district average for participation in the free lunch program is 78 percent; the state average is 49 percent. The school reports that 14 percent of its students are in ESL classes.

One-half of Westbury's students are immigrants from Central America and the Caribbean; the latter group is drawn largely from Haiti and the Dominican Republic.

Westbury administrators state emphatically that the school and district's most urgent and complex issue is providing their large population of immigrant students with the help they need to achieve academic success. The problems teachers must work on include: quickly assisting students' to understand, speak, read, and write English; integrating into an alien school environment many students whose schooling has been interrupted, sometimes for months or years. The school staff must alleviate as much as possible the physical, social, and emotional effects of poverty, and reach out to parents whose grasp of English is shaky and who tend to avoid contacts with school officials.

Assessment results for Westbury Middle School reflect a school that generally resembles the average test results for New York State; the school achieved a "Yes" on the Annual Yearly Progress (AYP) report for the total school and for all sub-groups. In grade eight, for example, on the State's English Language Assessment (ELA) students averaged 656, versus a state-wide average of 649. Grade eight math scores were 650, exactly matching the state average.

Westbury Middle School has a remarkable range of programs and interventions to boost the achievement levels of its students. The district has successfully sought grants from the state and private sources; the district's per-pupil expenditure of $21,500 far exceeds New York's average of $11, 900. Among the activities that level of funding plus faculty commitment have made possible are:

- The beginning and end of the school day are extended for tutorials and after-school activities, and students receive a substantial after-school snack. Tutorials are conducted on Saturdays.
- Teachers stay after school two hours each month (by contract) to tutor small groups of students.
- A Homework Center gives assistance three times a week.
- All written communications to parents are in English, Spanish, and Creole. A computerized translation service is available for parent meetings.
- Parents are invited to workshops that explain the nature, importance, and results of the state assessment program.
- The district offers English language programs for parents.
- Parents are urged to sign and support a contract that spells out academic and behavioral expectations for their children.
- Academic goals for the district are set on a four-year cycle. Principals meet three times a year with the superintendent to establish objectives for each building; progress is reviewed at midyear, and success in meeting goals is evaluated at the end of the school year. Administrators also make a yearly retreat at which they review goals from the previous year and reinstate or revise them for the future.

- Teachers work in two- to four-person teams, with common prep time and meetings of each team every other day. The school uses "looping" of teachers, that is, the teams stay with the same group of students for both seventh and eighth grade.
- The district employs a staff developer who works with grade six teachers on language arts and math.
- The district's curriculum mapping spells out how the school implements state standards. The maps are shared with parents to inform them of classroom expectations.

Lanier Middle School, Houston, Texas

Lanier is a charter school with some 1500 students in grades six through eight. Forty-four percent of its students are White, 31 percent Hispanic, 13 percent Black, and 11 percent Asian. Thirty percent of students are in the free and reduced lunch program.

On the Texas Assessment of Knowledge and Skills (TAKS) in 2008, 99 percent of Lanier's grade eight students were proficient in reading, versus the Texas average of 93 percent. In math, 93 percent of grade eight students were proficient versus the state average of 75 percent. The percentage of Lanier's proficient math students rose from 84 percent in 2005.

This school has received the Texas Gold Performance Awards in reading-language arts, mathematics, writing, science, social studies, and for student attendance.

The school takes great pride in its debate team. Lanier students won six consecutive national titles (2003–2008) in the National Junior Forensic League Championship.

The school's recognition for its sterling attendance record may be related to the very strict policies for tardiness to school or classes and for its efforts to combat truancy. The latter efforts include a threat of criminal charges against parents whose children are consistently truant.

Princeton Charter School, Princeton, New Jersey

The majority of students at Princeton Charter School (PCS) have a head start on academic achievement before they enroll in the school. The Princeton community is an affluent one, with a high proportion of parents who possess degrees in higher education, and with several major universities and colleges in or within a few miles of the town.

The Princeton Regional School System, consisting of four elementary schools, one middle school, and one high school, is highly regarded for its students' achievement. In this text, however, we focus on the local charter school, begun in 1997. The school draws on the same population as the regional schools but offers certain programs and emphases not available in the larger system. This description of PCS is more detailed than those for other middle schools (and perhaps less objective), because this author is so familiar with the PCS programs, having served several terms on that school's board and headed the school's committee on assessment.

PCS enrolls 344 students in grades K–8; in this profile, we will address only the middle school, grades five through eight (some 185 students).

Evidence of PCS's academic success includes scores on New Jersey's testing program. In 2008, 96 percent of grade eight students achieved proficiency in language arts, versus a statewide average of 81 percent. In mathematics, PCS eighth graders reached a 98 percent proficient rating, including 78 percent rated advanced proficient, versus 67 percent for the state. In science, PCS students ranked number one in New Jersey with 100 percent of grade eight students proficient, compared with an average of 84 percent for the state.

Since its inception in 1997, the school has also administered the Educational Records Bureau (ERB) Comprehensive Testing Program. These tests enable local schools to compare their students' performance with that of students in suburban schools and in independent schools, both more demanding criteria than national norms. The ERB tests are administered annually in October at PCS. A consultant presents the trustees with an analysis of the scores; the report follows each class as it moves through the grades, and shows comparisons with suburban and independent schools at the mean and at the 25th and 75th percentiles. PCS students match and in several subjects greatly exceed the norms for both comparison groups.

In mathematics, only five percent of suburban and independent students score as well as 25 percent of PCS eighth graders, while the lowest achieving 25 percent of the PCS population match the achievement of 60 percent of independent students, and 65 percent of suburban students.

On the ERB essay-writing assessment, only two percent of suburban and independent students score as well as the top 25 percent of PCS eighth graders. The lowest scoring 25 percent of PCS students equal the writing performance of 77 percent of suburban students and 75 percent of independent students.

In grades five through eight, students take final exams prepared by the faculty. Several class periods prior to the exams are devoted to reviewing the principal knowledge and skills taught in each course.

In 2005, PCS was named a National Blue Ribbon school. In the Great Schools rankings, the school received the top score of 10.

The school's guiding principle is a commitment to a rigorous academic program for every student in all disciplines. Students receive a full hour per day in English and mathematics, and 45 minutes daily in science, French or

Spanish, and social studies, plus art, music, and physical education. French classes begin in kindergarten, Spanish begins with grade three. Homework is assigned every day in English and math classes, and several times a week in other courses.

From grade four on, all PCS teachers are subject specialists, and students (or teachers) move from classroom to classroom during the day. In every discipline, emphasis is placed on following a prescribed sequence of content. The school's curriculum guide outlines the order in which teachers are to take up various topics, and the expectations for coverage of the curriculum.

In grades five through eight math classes are divided into several levels; on average, middle school math classes have 12 to 15 students in each section. Students are placed in math classes on the basis of their performance on five assessments and their teachers' observations. As slower students catch up with grade-level requirements, they are quickly moved up into the next section. The highest achieving students are challenged with advanced mathematics content. This flexibility serves the school's decision to advance the standards in the math textbook series by a full grade. That is, all third graders use the fourth grade text, and so on.

Even in an education-oriented community like Princeton, the schools have some students who fall behind in one or several subjects. Also, like most charter schools, PCS attracts parents whose children have learning problems in the schools in which they are enrolled. These students are the principal reason that PCS faculty members teach one less regular class per day than is customary for middle schools. As soon as a teacher reports a lagging student, his parents are informed, and he is assigned a faculty tutor. Sessions continue until the youngster can keep pace with his classmates; a few students require assistance for the entire school year. The school also has an after-school program for enrichment as well as for additional remedial tutoring, and for play time.

Like PCS's math classes, its middle school English classes also divide into smaller sections to promote discussion of readings, concentration on grammar, and greater opportunities for grading and reviewing writing assignments. All students have a silent reading period every day.

The school's charter documents and curriculum guide spell out expectations that grade eight students will write analytical, expository, and personal essays, using contextual evidence, and develop clear theses with solid supporting material.

"Milestones" are substantial, subject-related projects that all PCS students complete over the academic year. For example, in grade eight, students prepare a major paper on an historical subject. These papers must show substantial research about their content, be well written, and conform to the canons for a research paper. Both English and history teachers review the various stages of the grade eight milestone. Final papers are evaluated by community educators who are not PCS faculty members. Toward the end of the school year, certificates of achievement are awarded for each student's successful Milestone project.

Louis Pasteur Fundamental Intermediate School, Orangevale, California

This middle school on the fringe of a large city has some 850 students in grades seven and eight. Twenty percent of the students qualify for free/ reduced-fee lunches.

In 2006, Pasteur received a 783 on the Academic Performance Index (API), representing a 100-point gain over six years. The school meets all 13 criteria for Annual Yearly Progress.

In 2008 on the California Standards Test (CST), Pasteur's eighth graders scored at a 60 percent proficiency level; for California, the figure was 49 percent. In mathematics, 59 percent of Pasteur students achieved proficiency, compared with a state-wide average of 41 percent.

Technology supports learning at Pasteur in a major way. Students use spreadsheets to graph math problems, presentation software, word processing, and graphic organizer software. Map interpretation is aided by Global Positioning Satellite (GPS); GPSCaching is a scavenger hunt-type game that students play, using GPS receivers. The school has two technology laboratories, and three mobile labs to support and extend such activities.

Gen Y is a technology literacy program for seventh graders. Selected students receive nine weeks of training in using technology and troubleshooting. They then become "consultants" to the faculty, as they are paired with teachers to develop course-related supplementary technical material for classes.

PAWS is a character education program at LPFIS; since its inception, suspension rates have dropped 60 percent and expulsions decreased by 80 percent.

SUCCESSFUL PROGRAMS IN MIDDLE SCHOOLS

It is no surprise that what succeeds in elementary schools is often effective in middle schools as well. So, several of the practices listed below are common to both levels of schooling.

• A longer school day, week, and year: This practice requires substantial resources and commitment from administrators and teachers. But considerable increases in instructional hours have proven repeatedly to be associated with student growth in achievement.

Because the lengthening of instructional hours demands a large-scale commitment of teacher time and other resources, careful planning of the content and teaching strategies and frequent assessments are essential. Many students in these lengthened programs have not been successful in their regular classroom periods; simply reiterating content presentation and teaching methods seldom proves beneficial.

More days and longer hours of instruction are common features of charter schools, most of which serve disadvantaged students. A good example of this practice is seen in the profile of the KIPP Ujima Village Academy.

- High expectations and demanding programs for all students, with frequent informal assessments that are linked with readily available tutoring: This four-step formula is successfully applied at Princeton Charter School. The rigor of the school's academic program, including substantial homework assignments, has the support of parents. Students who are tutored move into a regular classroom schedule as soon as they catch up with their classmates. A few PCS students receive the year-round tutoring they require to keep up with their classmates.

- A primary emphasis on language learning: This practice pervades successful elementary schools and carries into strong middle schools. Reading instruction moves into more complex vocabulary, grammar, and syntax, and the analysis of literature. Writing instruction becomes more demanding in terms of mechanics, the development of style, and the use of various forms of written expression. Students' oral presentations of their work as well as reading aloud from poetry and passages from literature encourage growth in speaking skills.

  Among the profiled schools, an example of this dedication to language learning is Westbury Middle School. The large number of students who have little or no facility in English prompts Westbury teachers to make all-out efforts in helping their students learn to speak and understand, read and write English as quickly as possible.

  Von Steuben School, with assistance from their reading textbooks publisher, invested several years of staff training in the coordination and assessment of students' reading achievement.

- A systematic and tightly scheduled curriculum: As incoming middle schoolers leave their earlier self-contained classrooms and encounter a variety of teachers, it is essential that their instructors maintain the principal elements in a prescribed curriculum. Failure to do so can result in students arriving in the following year's courses with gaps in the knowledge and skills their new teachers expect them to have. The opposite effect is only slightly less disadvantageous: students repeat whole units they learned the previous year.

Maintaining an orderly approach to curriculum is made easier in Westbury Middle School, as teachers meet in teams every other day, and have prep time in common. The teams "loop," remaining with the same students in grades seven and eight.

- Resources: More funding is not, in itself, a guarantee of improvement, but schools whose students have high academic needs do require substantial resources to meet those needs. Two schools with high proportions of disadvantaged students that have enjoyed success in raising funds beyond the per-pupil allotments in their states and districts are Ujima Village School and Westbury Middle School. The former school has raised considerable funds from private sources, and Westbury has tapped both private and supplementary state funding.

- An extensive and sophisticated use of technology: At Louis Pasteur Fundamental Intermediate School, students' use of computer software is a beginning in realizing the potential for technology to upgrade the quality and efficiency of instruction. This school ingeniously attempts to resolve the sometimes unacknowledged problem that, even in middle school, many students are far more comfortable with computers than are their teachers. By pairing specially trained students with teachers, the students and faculty become partners in developing teaching materials. So, even apart from the acquisition of supplementary learning materials, teachers gain in comfort with technology, and students gain in self-esteem from their role as tutors.

- Professional development for teachers: As in both elementary and high schools, changes in the curriculum call for participation on the part of faculty. This is true for planning an innovation, but is equally or more essential for carrying out and constantly assessing the changes.

  At Von Steuben Middle School, professional development focuses on the basic need for teachers to coordinate their instruction with each other, and to ensure that the "real curriculum," that which is taught in the classrooms, connects by grade and subject level with state standards.

- Parental support and cooperation: Among the services Westbury Middle School provides for parents are written communications in Spanish and Creole as well as English, and the district's offering of English language classes for parents.

  The Ujima Academy holds meetings with parents before the school year begins. In these sessions school administrators explain the requirements for attendance and homework. Parents are asked for their commitment to support the school's policies in return for a promise that their children will be enabled to succeed academically.

Chapter 6

High Schools

INTRODUCTION

This is it! The final four of the 13-year Kindergarten through grade 12 sequence. For almost half of those who do graduate, grade 12 is the last year of formal schooling. For those who will not go on to higher education, high school is practically their last opportunity to gain academic knowledge and skills in a coherent, systematic way. The knowledge and skills these students take from high school will have a considerable impact on their working lives and their contribution to the nation's welfare.

As a principal in a typical U.S. high school looks over her incoming freshmen, what does she see?

1. A number of them who have developed systematic study skills, mastered and gone well beyond basic skills in reading, writing, and mathematics, and gained the emotional and social qualities that enable them to learn and allow others to do so. These are the students that teachers especially welcome to their classrooms and honors courses; such young people often find high school work grueling, but generally are pleased with their school and their prospects for college.
2. A second group of freshmen make up the majority of incoming students in most U.S. high schools. They have grasped enough elements of academic learning, social skills, and emotional development that they can begin high school courses. For these average students, the first year of high school is critical. If their teachers carefully monitor their classroom progress, it soon becomes evident which pupils need some academic and emotional support. Sadly, these average students frequently become lost

in schools' concern for those at the top and bottom levels of achievement. They slowly become invisible, classes are "boring," their grades decline, and school becomes, at best, a place to hang out with friends. When their names come up in the faculty room, one may hear, "He's just not motivated," an example of blaming the victim.

3. In a community or school with below-average socio-economic populations, a principal may also see records from middle school of near failure for anywhere from 20 to 50 percent of the incoming freshmen. Many of those low-achieving students have only a rudimentary grasp of basic skills, and usually have severe problems reading any but the simplest texts. Such students hate school and with good reason; it is a source of failure and humiliation for them. As teenagers, they tend to act out their frustrations in various ways, almost all disruptive to school order and destructive to their own futures.

Increasingly, states and school districts are requiring exams at the end of grade eight that will indicate students' readiness for high school courses. That requirement sounds like the beginning of a good idea, but the value of such exams depends on what the states and schools do with the results. The transition from middle to high school is the last chance for most failing students to learn what they need to succeed through high school and beyond.

Some districts have established a "Prep Year," in which incoming freshmen with low achievement are provided with intensive remedial work in language and math. Such programs allow students to move into regular classes as they are ready, and they are able to go on and graduate.

Many states and local school districts have increased the number of courses required for graduation; this increase has been most conspicuous in math and English. In 2005, 85 percent of high school graduates had taken four years of English. But only 64 percent had course work in grammar (down from 78 percent 10 years earlier). Sixty-two percent had course work in English composition (78 percent a decade earlier). The fallacy of legislatures or school boards mandating more courses without addressing the needs of students or specifying the course content is obvious. The error recalls the naïve belief by policy makers who are not educators that increasing funds to school districts without specifying how the money is to be spent and the expected outcomes will result in improved student achievement.

As with the earlier descriptions of elementary and middle schools, we will look at high schools whose students' academic achievement varies greatly. The socio-economic status of these schools and their communities ranges from very affluent, with high levels of parent education and involvement in their children's schooling, to more average communities, and to those that suffer from severe poverty and other disadvantages.

Before examining individual schools, let's again look briefly at the factors typically found in communities whose schools enroll students of superior academic achievement, and are largely missing in schools with predominantly disadvantaged populations:

- *Affluence* that is sufficient to provide resources and support to schools
- *High educational levels* of parents and the wider community
- *Expectations for high student achievement* on the part of parents and teachers
- *Resources,* both financial and professional that strengthen school programs

TEN SUCCESSFUL HIGH SCHOOLS

Bayside Senior High School (BSHS), Brevard County School District, Florida

Some 2,200 students are enrolled in BSHS, with 14 percent on free or reduced lunch. The socio-economic status of the district is described as low middle to middle class; some 23 percent of the residents are termed "economically disadvantaged." The school suffers from a high mobility rate; that factor, combined with its large enrollment, challenges Bayside's teachers and counselors to identify, maintain contact with, and provide timely help to struggling students.

BSHS receives Florida's top rating of "A" for academic achievement, with its strongest test scores in reading. In mathematics, the school average score is 16 percent above that of the state.

Both faculty and observers characterize Bayside's curriculum as a "rigorous, structured program." The school maintains a traditional six-period day, but embeds an extended time block for students enrolled in an intensive reading/English course.

Students who score at the 50th percentile on the PSAT and achieve a GPA of 3.0 or better are eligible for courses for gifted students, AP Prep, and AP courses.

Bayside has a full-time enrollment program with Brevard Community College. The school says that its "ultimate goal is students achieving an Associate in Arts and a high school diploma on graduation day."

Palmer High School (PHS), Colorado Springs, Colorado

Palmer High School has some 2000 students in its grades 9 through 12. Some 27 percent of the student body receives free or reduced-fee lunches. When school officials correlated participation in the subsidized lunch program with students' grades, they discovered that those in the lunch program performed far below the school's average achievement—about half as well in some subjects and grades as those not eligible for the lunch program.

The school is rated "4" (high) on a five-point scale based on Colorado's Student Assessment Program and on ACT results. The state requires the ACT for all grade 11 students. Palmer students score slightly above the state average on the ACT composite score and equal the ACT national average.

In 2008, grade nine reading scores at Palmer showed 79 percent at or above the proficient level versus the state mean of 66 percent. In grade nine math, 54 percent of Palmer's students were at or above proficient, compared with the state average of 38 percent. Grade 10 scores show a similar pattern, with 71 percent of Palmer students scoring proficient or above in reading, versus 66 percent for the state. In math, 48 percent of Palmer test takers scored at or above proficient, as opposed to 30 percent state-wide.

A major program at Palmer is Response to Intervention (RTI). This program systematically identifies students' learning needs and provides small-group instruction several times a week, with monitoring and frequent assessment; teaching is adjusted as indicated by the assessments. Instruction in RTI begins with monitoring and support for all students. When more intervention is indicated, learning specialists are introduced to aid classroom teachers in monitoring and assisting struggling students. The third level of RTI involves a comprehensive evaluation to determine an individual student's eligibility for special education.

Adlai Stevenson High School (ASHS), Lincolnshire, Illinois

This school in a suburb of Chicago has some 4,500 students in grades 9 through 12. The percentage of economically disadvantaged students is 2.4 percent, and 4.6 percent of the student body are African-American or Hispanic.

Some 63 percent of adults in the Lincolnshire community possess at least a bachelor's degree, versus the state average of 29.8 percent.

Results on the state assessment program for this high school are as follows:

Reading: 84.4 percent are proficient versus the state average of 54 percent. Sixty percent of ESL students at Stevenson are proficient readers; 63.5 percent of those designated economically disadvantaged achieve proficiency.

In mathematics, 86.3 percent of Stevenson students are proficient, compared with a state-wide average of 52.7 percent.

At Stevenson, 61 percent of the entire student body participates in the Advanced Placement Program; the rate of AP exams per test-taker is 4.7; the school's AP pass rate (grade 3 or better) is 85.6 percent. Stevenson also offers the International Baccalaureate and other honors courses. The graduation rate at Stevenson is 96.5 percent; that for the state is 85.9.

In 2009, Stevenson was designated "One of America's Best High Schools" by U.S. News and World Report. The school is a four-time winner of the U.S. Department of Education's Blue Ribbon Award.

A school with the resources and student population that Stevenson possesses has a variety of interventions and many special programs and services, including the Professional Learning Community (PLC), a nationally recognized professional development movement. Another of Stevenson's strengths is its focus on maintaining a coherent instructional program through curriculum mapping.

At Stevenson, the faculty "owns" the curriculum, that is, the teachers create for each grading period, clearly stated, measurable standards and objectives that students will attain, including critical thinking skills, reading, and writing standards. Teachers then devise and administer common assessment measures for those standards. Teachers and administrators meet to discuss the results of the assessment measures and plan improvement in the curriculum—the content and teaching strategies for their courses.

Montgomery Township High School (MTHS), Skillman, New Jersey

Montgomery Township High School has some 1620 students: 1210 are white, 337 Asian, 37 African-American, and 37 Hispanic. Two percent of the enrolled students are eligible for free or reduced-fee lunch; in the township, 1.5 percent of the families are below the poverty line, and the median income per family is $129,000. The township's population has grown 140 percent between 1990 and 2006; the increase in K–12 numbers is from 1590 students in 1992 to 4,924 in 2005.

On New Jersey's 2008 High School Proficiency Assessment (HSPA), MTHS's grade 11 students achieved 97 percent proficiency in language arts, versus New Jersey's average of 83 percent. In the same year and grade, Montgomery students scored 96 percent proficient in math, compared with 75 percent state-wide. The school's assessment results are especially noteworthy when one considers that, on the language arts exam, 46.6 percent of Montgomery's students scored at the "Advanced Proficient" level; in math, 55 percent of Montgomery students were "Advanced Proficient."

The school's results on the Advanced Placement examinations are equally stellar, with 41 percent of the test-takers receiving the top grade of "5," and 89 percent attaining a grade of "3" or more.

Montgomery's average SAT score of 1755 (V and M) is 244 points above the national average. The school has 10 semi-finalists and 38 commended scholars in the National Merit competition. The graduation rate is 99.4 percent.

The school receives the highest grade (10) from the Great Schools rating service.

MTHS has a substantial commitment to science education, extending beyond the usual science courses. Students are very active in the Science Olympiad, the Science League, the Science Bowl, and FIRST robotics. Students can choose programs in architecture, TV production, and computer languages and applications.

MTHS students have also compiled outstanding records in various sports; their boys or girls teams are state title holders or finalists in baseball, softball, lacrosse, cross country, hockey, and tennis.

The school places a strong emphasis on community service, with numerous clubs and projects devoted to that purpose.

Boston Collegiate Charter School (BCCS), Dorchester, Massachusetts

BCCS was founded in 1998 and has expanded rapidly to its current enrollment of 460 students in grades five through twelve. Forty-one percent of the students are at or below the poverty line; 17 percent are in Individual Education Plans (IEP). The present student body is made up of 62 percent White students, 28 percent African-Americans, and 8 percent Hispanic. Ten years earlier, the school enrolled twice its current number of White students, and only five percent Black and two percent Hispanic students.

In 2008, 100 percent of BCCS 10th graders passed the English portion of the Massachusetts Comprehensive Assessment System (MCAS); over the last six years, 99 percent of BCCS sophomores passed that English exam.

BCCS is the only public school in Massachusetts where 100 percent of 10th graders passed the mathematics section of the MCAS for six consecutive years.

On the SAT I, in 2008, BCCS average verbal score was 494; in mathematics the average was 545. This compares with the Boston school system's scores of 434 in verbal, and 451 in math.

For six consecutive years, 100 percent of the senior class was accepted into college. For two years in a row, BCCS received the National Silver Medal for its gains in student achievement.

BCCS credits much of its students' success to a large-scale and carefully designed system for assessing students' academic progress. Among the features of that system are:

- "Quiz Days," on which the entire school participates in various oral assessments.
- Faculty members develop math and English tests for frequent formative and summative course assessments, and for standardized test preparation.
- Final exams are mandatory in all grades.
- BCCS is a member of the Massachusetts Public School Performance (MPSP), a consortium of schools that creates math and reading assessments that are aligned with state standards. Member schools compare data across schools and share best practices.

Parents are involved in BCCS through the Collegiate Connection. They volunteer at the school, raise funds, and host parent workshops.

Reitz Memorial High School (RMHS), Evansville, Indiana

Some 840 students are enrolled in Reitz Memorial High School, which is part of the Evansville Catholic School System. Student participation in the free/reduced lunch program is three percent, versus a state average of 42 percent. Annual tuition at RMHS is $3,970.

Evansville's population is 121,000. Some 24 percent of its citizens possess college degrees, compared with an Indiana average of 20 percent. In median household income, Evansville's $32,700 lags well behind the state average of $42,650. Almost 14 percent of the city's population is below the poverty line, with 19 percent of children under 18 years of age falling below that level.

The 2009 report on Indiana's state-wide assessment program shows RMHS grade 10 students at 94 percent proficiency in language arts, compared with the state average of 78 percent. In mathematics, RMHS sophomores averaged 93 percent proficiency. In 2009, 91 percent passed both state-wide language arts and math tests, compared with the Indiana average of 59 percent.

In grade 12, SAT scores for RMHS students averaged 531 verbal, and 538 mathematics. Averages across the state were 496 and 493 respectively.

Reitz Memorial's graduation rate is 98.9 percent; ninety-one percent of graduates enroll in four-year colleges. In 2002, the school received a national Blue Ribbon School Award.

In this sports-minded state, community support for the school is bolstered by an outstanding record in competitive athletics. In recent years, the school has repeatedly won state titles in seven sports; in 2007 and 2008, the boys' soccer team won the national title.

The school has developed a Bridge Program with the University of Evansville. College courses are taught by high school teachers at the school. College credit is awarded for students who satisfactorily complete the courses; these credits are recorded for University of Evansville transcripts.

Hamilton High School (HHS), Chandler, Arizona

Hamilton is a high school with over 3,000 students. Chandler is a Phoenix suburb that has seen explosive growth, from a population of 30,000 in 1980 to some 250,000 today. The median household income is $69,000; 4.6 percent of families are below the poverty line. At HHS, 6.3 percent of students qualify for free/reduced lunches, versus a state average of 41 percent.

On the 2008 Arizona Instrument to Measure Standards (AIMS) tests, grade 10 students at HHS scored at 87 percent proficient versus a state average of 73 percent. In writing, Hamilton sophomores were rated 91 percent proficient compared with 68 percent statewide; in mathematics, 87 percent were proficient, versus 67 percent throughout Arizona.

In 2005, Hamilton was rated a Blue Ribbon Lighthouse School. The school receives the top score of 10 on the Great Schools rating.

The sports program at HHS is a major element in the school curriculum, and a source of pride to the school community. A more unusual feature of Hamilton (and several other Phoenix area schools) is the Hamilton Prep School, a spinoff from the larger high school. Hamilton Prep, begun in 2008–09, will eventually enroll grades 7–12. The prep school will be strongly academic in orientation, with an all-honors curriculum. The new school's goal is rigorous preparation for college. As one of the deans said, "We're a year ahead (of Hamilton High School), and we follow a quicker pace." The prep school is distinctive for its smaller classes and strict discipline; school uniforms are mandatory. The resources of the larger "parent" school are available to the prep school.

Carolina High School and Academy (CHSA), Greenville, South Carolina

Carolina High School and Academy enrolls 730 students in grades 9–12. Greenville's population is 56,000, with a large minority population; recently, the area has experienced heavy international immigration. The median household income is $36,000.

On the South Carolina High School Assessment Program (HSAP), CHSA students showed considerable growth as well as some variation for the period 2004–08. In 2004, 71 percent of the graduates were proficient in English, and 50 percent in math. Just two years later, 87 percent of CHSA students were proficient in English, and 76 percent in math. However, in 2007–08, the percentage of students proficient in English dipped to 79 percent.

The school is listed by the Southern Regional Education Board among the "High Schools That Work."

CHSA has a curricular focus on pre-engineering and on health care careers. The school has strong participation in the Advanced Placement Program, and has a dual-enrollment program with local community colleges.

The school uses the Promethean Board, a high tech aid to instruction in mathematics.

Grover Cleveland High School (GCHS), Resada, California

Resada is a community of about 80,000 (in year 2000) in the San Fernando Valley. GCHS is part of the Los Angeles Unified School District. The school has over 4,000 students in grades nine through twelve. Fifty-eight percent of the students are Hispanic, 18 percent are White, 13 percent Asian, and 9 percent are African-American. Sixty-six percent of the students are eligible for free or reduced-fee lunches.

On the California Standards Tests (CST) GCHS students show superior achievement in mathematics, and equal or exceed the state average in English Language Learning. For example, in 2008, grade 10 algebra scores show 64 percent of GCHS proficient, compared with 36 percent state-wide. In the same year and grade, 46 percent of GCHS students were proficient in English Language Learning, versus a 41 percent state average.

In 2005, the school received the California Distinguished School Award. GCHS has a rating of seven (of a possible 10) from Great Schools. The same service assigns a four to the Los Angeles Unified District.

The very large student body at Grover Cleveland High School is divided into eight smaller learning communities. One of these communities, the School for Advanced Studies, is intended to challenge high-achieving students with honors-level English and biology classes in grades nine and ten. Students in this learning community must take their first Advanced Placement course in grade 10. A related small community, the Humanities Magnet Core, is a rigorous four-year program; Advanced Placement history and English are mandatory for the junior and senior years.

GCHS prides itself on its Media Academy. The Academy's curriculum is intended to develop traditional, digital, and audio-visual communication skills in the arts and sciences. The sequence of courses begins in grade nine or ten, and continues to graduation. The Academy's program has received numerous awards for its film and television productions.

Among GCHS's excellent math programs is a two-year instructional sequence that moves students into calculus BC by their junior year.

School for the Talented and Gifted (TAG), Dallas, Texas

TAG is a magnet school in the Dallas Independent School District; the school enrolls 200 students in grades 9–12. Twenty-nine percent of the students are economically disadvantaged. The racial makeup of the school generally reflects the Dallas population, with 42 percent of students White, 28 percent Hispanic, 24 percent Black, and 6 percent Asian.

TAG was named "Best School in the United States" by Newsweek magazine in 2006 and 2007; in 2008, it was number two. In the U.S. News and World Report rating of magnet schools, TAG was number three in the country.

According to the College Board, TAG has the highest passing rate in the world for Advanced Placement (AP) Computer Science and for Human Geography.

The school is ranked first in Texas for overall passing rates since 2001. In language arts, mathematics, science, and social studies, 100 percent of TAG students in grades 9, 10, and 11 were classified as proficient on the state assessment program.

The number of students in classes at TAG ranges from 5 to 17.

The Texas Education Agency (TEA) requires that seniors complete an "Exit-level Project" that employs outside mentoring, with projects judged at the state level. The TEA's Advanced High School Program is enhanced at TAG by pre-AP and AP curricula. Advanced students can take the AP Calculus BC exam, and the Independent Study in Mathematics program includes numbers theory and linear algebra.

SUCCESSFUL PROGRAMS IN HIGH SCHOOLS

Among the ten high schools profiled here, probably only Carolina High School and Academy enrolls a majority of seriously disadvantaged student population. Other schools—Bayside, Palmer, and TAG—draw on communities and families that are more average in resources. Three schools—Adlai Stevenson, Montgomery Township, and Hamilton—receive their students from relatively affluent communities and families.

The criticism voiced repeatedly about the overall quality of U.S. high school education does not apply to the schools described here. Certainly, negative comments can be made about many schools with highly disadvantaged student populations, but not about Carolina High School and Academy. The belief that virtually none of our students are being adequately taught is belied by the outstanding schools alluded to below. And at least some schools whose resources and achievements fall between the extremes cannot be termed mediocre, as is evidenced by schools like Bayside, and Palmer.

The programs and interventions that flourish in the listed high schools are these:

- *Provisions for high achievers*
  Bayside Senior High School must deal with the handicap of high student mobility. Despite this problem, the school provides a strong education for all students, with special provisions for gifted and talented students. The school requires a threshold level of achievement on the PSAT and grade point average for its special courses, as well as for Advanced Placement Prep and AP courses. Bayside also partners with Brevard Community College in allowing its more able students to pursue an Associate in Arts degree simultaneously with their high school diploma.

  Dual enrollment provisions with local colleges are a feature of several other schools with high-achieving students. Students at Reitz Memorial High School are treated as full enrollees at the nearby University of Evansville, and their credits become part of their college transcript. Carolina Academy also has a close partnership with local colleges.

  The student body at Montgomery Township High School is remarkably advanced in academic achievement. In addition to an extensive AP program, the school encourages its many high-achieving students to participate in extra-classroom science programs, including one in robotics.

  High-aspiring students at Arizona's Hamilton High School can shift to an alternative school with very demanding expectations and courses. This "school within a school" offers only honors level courses, while its students can participate in many of the activities of the larger school.

  The School for the Talented and Gifted (TAG) in Dallas has repeatedly received national recognition for the high level of its AP scores, and the rigor of courses that its talented student body can enter.
- *Provisions for low achievers*
  Carolina High School and Academy focuses its students on career opportunities in their early high school years. Programs in pre-engineering and health care, plus dual-enrollment opportunities with local community

colleges, enable students to envision and prepare for careers that offer them important and remunerative work.

At Palmer High School, students who are struggling in their courses benefit from the school's Response to Intervention (RTI) program. The program's structure insures prompt intervention with frequent assessment of progress; if a student's achievement continues to lag, the intensity of interventions moves to a higher level.

* *Faculty control of curriculum*
Each grading period, the teachers at Adlai Stevenson High School create the standards and learning objectives their students are expected to master, and devise common assessment measures for determining student mastery. Assessment results are discussed in meetings of teachers and administrators, and curriculum improvements are agreed upon.

* *Sports Programs*
By contributing to students' and communities' pride in their schools, outstanding sports programs bolster academic achievement in a number of successful high schools. Of course, over-hyped sports programs can also deflect attention and resources from a school's primary purpose, but this is not the case in schools like Montgomery Township, Reitz Memorial, and Hamilton.

* *Continued programs*
Some of the curriculum interventions that succeed in elementary and middle school are adopted by and adapted to high schools. These programs try to remediate deficiencies in student achievement, or to prevent these problems from beginning.

Increasingly, high schools are cooperating with middle schools to determine students' readiness for succeeding in their freshman year. When participating high schools identify the demands of freshman year and middle school educators evaluate their students' abilities to undertake those challenges, instruction and counseling can be initiated in grade eight and continued into the freshman year.

The overriding emphasis on language skills that characterizes successful elementary and middle schools carries into successful high schools. These schools provide the advanced levels of literary interpretation and writing skills that are critical preparation for college.

Regrettably, most high schools do not provide the skilled, intensive teaching that students with minimal reading and writing ability desperately need. A few schools have accepted the realities of social promotion in elementary and middle schools and added remedial teachers of reading and writing to their staffs.

A new program, Word Generation, addresses the need for supplementary literacy instruction in middle and high schools. A problem identified by the program's originator, Strategic Research Education Partnership, NA is that students sometimes misunderstood or ignored academic words and phrases commonly found in their school texts. SRES devised vocabulary lessons taught each day by teachers across middle school curricula. Early results are promising, especially for ESL students.

Chapter 7

Three School Districts

INTRODUCTION

The three preceding chapters concentrate on individual schools, their characteristics, and how they have raised their students' achievement. For principals and teachers, their own schools are the focus of concern, and other similar schools offer the best promise of interventions that would work for them.

Most public schools are units within larger systems; their curricula and most of their programs are specified by their school district. To examine a range of curricula and programs, it is useful now to consider three school systems that are very different from one another in location, students, and resources, but all of which enjoy considerable success in raising students' academic outcomes. Obviously, an individual school faculty would have to consider the extent to which programs in these systems seem to fit their students' needs.

SUCCESSFUL DISTRICTS

The Disadvantaged: Brownsville Independent School District

In 2008, the Brownsville, Texas, Independent School District won the Broad Prize for its success in raising student achievement for a greatly disadvantaged population. The Broad Foundation annually awards one million dollars to the urban school district demonstrating the greatest overall performance in improving student achievement, while reducing the achievement gap between impoverished minority students and those who enjoy greater advantages. (For past years' awards see "Broad Prize Winners" online.) Competition for the prize is fierce, and in evaluating the applications, the Foundation requires

multiple sources and evidence of success: these include significant improvement in test scores and other recorded indicators, site visits, observations,
and interviews.

Brownsville, Texas, is situated on the U.S. Mexican border, and has
one of the poorest urban populations in America. The district has 49,000
students, 94 percent of whom are eligible for free or reduced-fee lunches; the
Broad report characterizes the community as one of "stark poverty." Many
Brownsville parents are migrant workers whose children suffer various handicaps to school learning, often including interrupted schooling while their families work in other regions of the U. S. Forty-three percent of Brownsville's
students speak English as a second language, an additional handicap.

The Broad Foundation cited four reasons for the Brownsville award:

1. The district outperforms other similar Texas districts in reading and math
    at all levels.
2. The district shows substantial improvement in the academic achievement
    of ethnic and low-income sub-groups.
3. Between 2004 and 2007, Brownsville reduced the achievement gap
    between Hispanic students and the average for White students by
    12 percentage points in middle school math, and between low income and
    non-low income students by nine percent in high school reading.
4. The district has strong district-wide policies and practices, including pro-
    visions for individual and school accountability.

What are the programs and interventions that have proven so successful in
Brownsville, a district that faces many severe challenges?

- The district has aligned its curriculum and assessment system with the state
  standards found in the Texas Essential Knowledge and Skills (TEKS). A
  uniform pace of delivery is prescribed for scope and sequence across subject areas and grade levels.
- Each year, representatives from every professional staff level—teachers
  through area superintendents—participate in a formal curriculum review.
- Students needing additional instruction and practice in English meet at the
  district's Saturday Academies. The district holds summer intervention programs; specialized computer software programs and after-school tutoring
  are also available.
- "Success is never an accident" is a district motto. District-wide benchmark
  assessments are given twice yearly in core academic subjects for grades
  three through twelve. Teachers use the assessment results to identify instructional objectives that are not being met satisfactorily.

- Parents are offered the options of enrolling their children in a transitional program with instruction in Spanish and English and a strong ESL component, or a dual-immersion program with instruction in both languages.
- Brownsville makes extensive and sophisticated use of computers both in classrooms and in computer laboratories. The district also partners with city facilities like the public libraries for after-school student access to computers. These opportunities are critically important if Brownsville students are to have access to computers, since many of their parents cannot afford to purchase one for their homes. The district is also buying computer hardware to enable students to practice for and take standardized tests online.

The Advantaged: Montgomery County School District, Maryland

Montgomery County Schools enroll some 140,000 students in 199 schools, making the district the eighth largest in the U.S. The county is essentially a suburb of Washington DC; over the last few decades, the area has moved from affluent, homogeneous communities to a multi-cultural mix of families, with more than 160 nationalities speaking 120 different languages. Some 32,000 (23 percent) of its students are on free or reduced-fee lunch. However, the district overall retains much of its characteristic as an area of well-educated parents who are strongly interested in school affairs.

According to the superintendent, "We have three-quarters of our kids testing at or above the national averages for the second grade on standardized tests, and we have all minorities and subgroups above the national average."

In grade five reading (2007), 83.4 percent of Montgomery students were proficient versus the state average of 76.7. In mathematics, 84 percent of Montgomery students were proficient versus the state's 78.3 percent. Both scores improved between 2003 and 2007: reading moved from the 75th percentile to the 83rd, and math from the 68th to the 84th percentile.

Thirty-two of Montgomery's schools have been recognized as National Blue Ribbon Schools.

A district of this size has many programs to maintain and raise students' achievement. Among the most notable ones are:

- At the elementary school level, the district sponsors' interventions (tutoring, extra instructional time) that focus intensely on the five fundamental components of reading: phonemic awareness, phonics, fluency, vocabulary, and comprehension.

- At the middle and high school levels, students enrolled in Program Read 180 receive 90 minutes daily of language instruction in addition to their English classes. The district also offers a College Prep Literacy Program.
- Montgomery has three magnet schools: one specializes in advanced mathematics, advanced computer science, digital design, and gaming; a second teaches the performing arts, communications, and the humanities; the third magnet school teaches math and science focused on robotic engineering and aerospace.
- Accelerated and enriched instruction is provided at all three levels of schooling.

The Challenged: Chugach School District, Anchorage, Alaska

This district gives new meaning to the term "rural schools." Chugach enrolls just 214 students who are spread over 22,000 square miles in isolated areas of south central Alaska. Chugach schools enroll students from preschool age to 21 year olds; instruction is delivered personally or electronically in schools, workplaces, community centers, and homes on a 24 hours, seven days a week basis. Alaskan native minorities make up 50 percent of the student body, three-quarters of students are below the poverty line, and the areas served by the district have a 50 percent unemployment rate.

In 1994, the average student in the district was three years behind grade level in reading. By 2008, the district's average score had moved from the 28th percentile to the 71st percentile in reading, and from the 53rd to the 78th percentile in math. Chugach students top Alaska's average by eight percent in reading, 17 percent in math, and 35 percent in writing.

The district received the Baldridge National Quality Award in 2001.

The district employs an elaborate standards-based intervention model that is imitated in other states, including New Mexico and Washington.

All Chugach students have an Individual Learning Plan. As they become proficient in a course, students are moved to the next level. Some students graduate from high school at age 14, others at age 21.

An important goal in Chugach: "Students will understand, preserve, and appreciate their own language and the culture and heritage of others."

The enormous spread of the district encourages intensive use of technology. All students have a laptop computer, enabling them to connect with school programs any time and from almost any location. The superintendent and senior leaders confer twice monthly with remote sites by teleconference. Teachers have 30 days of in-service instruction per year.

The district's program is laid out in great detail in a CD ROM, "Guide to Reinventing Schools."

SUCCESSFUL PROGRAMS IN SCHOOL DISTRICTS

The three profiled districts differ widely in their communities, resources, and students. They share a commitment to student achievement; the programs they have initiated exemplify and further that commitment.

Concentrated efforts in teaching English language skills characterize both the Montgomery County District and that of Brownsville. Montgomery begins its language interventions in the early grades of elementary school with a focus on the fundamental components of reading. But the intensive teaching of reading continues; several more English language programs follow in middle and high schools.

In the Brownsville District, the basics of reading and writing are supplemented by coaching and practice in speaking and listening skills.

An extensive and sophisticated use of technology is seen in Brownsville's programs for making computers accessible and using them to practice for and take assessments. For still other reasons, Chugach has made a virtue of necessity as their computer network gives access to instruction for students and schools spread thinly over an enormous geographic area.

Extensive professional development activities are in place in these disparate districts. In Montgomery County, such activities help to maintain quality and a degree of uniformity within a staff of several thousand teachers. In Chugach, the unusually large number of days devoted to teacher instruction and conferencing reflects the need to overcome the isolation that teachers experience in a district challenged by distances and climate.

Individualized Learning Plans in the Chugach District are the system's intelligent and humane way of responding to the challenges of a severely disadvantaged student population. Students are moved through the system as they demonstrate mastery, but do not face many deadlines for completing levels of schooling, including graduation from high school.

Chapter 8

Evaluating Curriculum Changes

We refer several times to educators' sometimes skeptical reactions when they hear of schools that report interventions and curriculum changes that substantially contribute to student achievement. A reasonable question they may ask is, "How do we know those programs really work?" The appropriate, even essential response to that question is: "By assessing and evaluating the program outcomes."

Curriculum evaluation involves analyzing the results of assessments, drawing inferences, making judgments about what the assessment data tell us, and deciding what to do—revise some content or approach to a lesson, assign a grade, and so on.

Assessment, which precedes evaluation, is the process of gathering data, organizing and classifying it, then summarizing the results. The terms *assessment* and *evaluation* are sometimes used interchangeably, but it's important to realize that results of an assessment, no matter how comprehensive and well-designed, are not an evaluation. Tests are a form of assessment that contribute to, but do not substitute for the professional judgment of teachers and administrators that evaluation requires.

The most important question with which to initiate any assessment-evaluation plan is "How will I use the results?" Responses to that question will vary according to the nature of the curriculum change under evaluation, but in general assessment and evaluation can be used for *formative* or *summative* purposes.

Formative Curriculum Evaluation

Formative evaluation is meant to *inform,* to tell us what elements in the curriculum seem to be working well, and to indicate how less effective elements can be improved. Formative evaluation is usually informal. It gives teachers and students frequent glimpses of how well learning is progressing, and what works in the curriculum.

Formative evaluation acknowledges what every good teacher knows; it's not enough to say, "I teach to the state standards and my lesson plans follow the district curriculum guidelines, so what else do I need to know?" Some useful additional questions are: "Are my students mastering the essential material?" and, "Can they use the information and apply the skills they have learned?" Then follows the action question: "How can I modify my curriculum and lesson plans to enhance student achievement?"

The qualities of formative evaluation are as follows:

1. It is frequent, occurring almost constantly in a lively classroom.
2. It is informal, using even casual observation on the teacher's part.
3. It provides immediate feedback to teachers about their students' learning, and to students about their grasp of the course content.
4. Its primary purpose is to adjust what is being taught—the curriculum—to students' needs, not to give grades or create records.
5. Formative evaluation primarily provides information for incremental changes in teaching; it is not appropriate for high-stakes decisions about students or the curriculum.

Summative Curriculum Evaluation

Summative evaluation differs from formative evaluation first, in its purposes and uses: to facilitate a judgment or decision about a major element in the curriculum. Second, summative evaluation requires a degree of rigor that formative evaluation does not. An evaluation that leads to important decisions should be as valid and reliable as possible. An example is an end-of-course exam that contributes heavily to students' final grades. A larger scale example of summative assessment and evaluation is the state examinations that determine schools' rankings, whether they are "passing" or "failing" schools, and prescribe remedial efforts that failing schools must undertake.

Summative assessments are typically lengthier than their formative counterparts because they should cover all the major elements of a unit or course, and because the degrees of validity and reliability can be strengthened by a large sampling of the domain to be measured. Summative assessments are definitely not casual or informal, because much rides on their outcomes. If a decision is to be made on the basis of a single score on a summative assessment (rarely a good idea), the measurement qualities of that assessment must be very strong.

In chapter four, we profile Garfield Elementary School in Long Beach, California. Among the curriculum interventions that Garfield uses in compiling its enviable record of student achievement is the designation of three periods a week in grades four and five for specialists to provide small classes with direct instruction in writing. In terms of instructional time and teacher resources, these special writing sessions represent a substantial outlay of resources for the school and the district. The faculty, as well as local and district administrators want to know whether the results justify continuing the program. That intent answers our basic query, "How will the results of the evaluation be used?"

A summative evaluation of Garfield's special writing program begins with the answer to another basic question: "What are the program's objectives?" Chief among them, presumably, is the improvement of participating students' writing skills. "Improvement" suggests measurable gain, so the school's faculty must first determine the status of students entering the program. Garfield's program extends over grades four and five; the best measure of program effects will come from determining the same students' level of writing at the beginning of grade four and the end of grade five. Two years of intervention should provide fairly reliable evidence of gains for a class. Note that the same students should be assessed. That is, the calculation ought not be by grade: this year's fourth graders versus last years' fourth graders, but rather a two-year measure of the same students as they move through grades four and five.

Tests and Other Measures

Both standardized tests and teachers' own classroom tests can be used to assess writing progress, but those measures alone will not tell the entire story that a summative evaluation should provide. Some examples of questions that can yield further useful information are: Do these students write more and better in other classes and in later grades? (Use teacher interviews); Do students seem to enjoy writing more? (Ask them); Do language arts teachers from outside the school see marked improvement in samples of students' writing over two years? Do parents notice any difference in their children's skills or attitudes about writing? The data gathered from the sources just mentioned sound "soft," and they are; they're not sufficiently reliable or convincing to justify a decision about continuing or radically modifying a writing program. It's true that a summative judgment based solely on parents' opinions, for example, would not be justified. Rather, program evaluations should use all available measures, cumulate the results, then reach a decision about a program. It's also true that a well-designed, valid, and reliable test of writing is the best single source of data on Garfield's program results.

But if good tests supply good data, why not simply rely on test scores alone to understand program effects?

- As mentioned earlier, the common practice of comparing students in a specific grade over several years does not yield information on the same students. That is, comparing results in this year's fifth grade with those of last year requires measuring two different groups of students. (Last year's fifth graders are now in grade six.)
- Gains or losses in tested achievement are often less than meets the eye; they are not statistically significant. The differences may be due to chance and could disappear or even reverse on another similar test. Note that even the best crafted tests have a margin of error.
- Most test scores are reported as averages. Without knowing the range of scores for various groups within the total test population, we don't know how well the highest or lowest achieving students are doing. If, for example, a school institutes an extra period a day of reading instruction in grade three, and test results show an average gain among third graders of two grade levels over a school year, it's possible that the program substantially improved scores among the least able readers while showing little improvement among those already reading at grade level or above—or vice-versa.
- Certain qualities that bear on students' writing achievement cannot be measured by written exams, for example, students' attitudes toward reading: do they feel it's important? Enjoyable? Do they voluntarily read at home? Do they enjoy certain types of reading, such as science fiction or biographies of heroes? Do they feel they are improving in their reading skills? Positive student attitudes can contribute to stronger student performance.

If tests are an important but insufficient source of information about a program's success, what are other measures that might be used? We have mentioned some questions that could be posed to various sources of information about the program. Many other instruments and techniques exist for assessing student achievement, including check lists, anecdotal records, specimen records, event sampling, and so on. (For detailed information on these techniques, see Wortham, 2005, pp. 97–195). We especially recommend an obvious, simple, and important measure, that of teachers' classroom observation.

Students' performance is the most important measure of the effectiveness of a curriculum. Classroom teachers can contribute significantly to an assessment of student learning because they have so many opportunities to observe students' performances. Much of this observation is casual and informal, but maximum benefit is derived if, for at least some of these observations, teachers create simple rating scales and periodically record students' performances. When students are making oral presentations, such an observation record is quick to use and provides enough specific information for feedback. Even written assignments can be assessed with such a simple record. For example, teachers could select major elements of writing skills—organization, support, grammar, spelling and punctuation, word choice, and overall development. For each element, teachers prepare a three-point scale (for example, 1—Unsatisfactory, 2—Satisfactory, 3—Excellent) with a brief description or evidence of the quality represented by each scale point. Several times over a grading period, teachers jot down the number that corresponds to each student's writing performance.

A great advantage of observation is that teachers assess student performance under natural conditions, without the stress that accompanies a major examination. A drawback is the danger of depending on a single or brief observation, which will be of doubtful reliability. But a record of multiple observations is a powerful measure of student performance.

Qualities of Program Assessment

The assessment that precedes evaluation should be examined for three qualities: validity, reliability, and efficiency. Briefly, an assessment is *valid* to the extent it measures what it claims to measure. A writing test should contain questions or problems that demonstrate students' mastery of the knowledge and skills of good writing. More specifically, validity refers to how the results of the assessment are used, that is, what inferences can a teacher properly draw on the basis of the assessment results? What decisions about a class or an individual student may a teacher make based on the test results? When multiple sources of information about a program are employed, each measure may possess only modest validity; it is insufficient of itself to justify a major decision. But an accumulation of results from various measures will yield more robust information for summative assessments and evaluations.

Reliability refers to the consistency of results. Overheard in the faculty room: "I don't know what happened to Marita on yesterday's exam. She almost always receives the highest grade in my class, but yesterday she had one of the lowest scores." We can think of at least two explanations for this not so uncommon happening. One is that Marita was having one of those bad days that occasionally plague us all. It's also possible that the test, not the student is unreliable. If several of his better students do poorly on an exam, a teacher should ask, "Did I devise a good test? Did it include enough questions on important material of the course? Were my directions and time allocations adequate? And, did I teach the material?"

Efficiency in an assessment means that it yields useful information with the least possible demand on students and teachers. Both validity and reliability can be improved by increasing the coverage, that is, adding more and more test items that measure more and more of the domain to be examined. But the amount of time students spend on testing, as well as the time teachers spend in devising and grading the results are constraints on the length of any exam.

Certainly, if a test result contributes substantially to a major decision about a program's or a student's future, it should be as valid and reliable as is reasonably possible. Most standardized tests include many items, and demand hours of test time; consider the time required for most state testing programs, or for the SAT or ACT examinations. The time spent on these exams is one objection teachers and students have to them. However, a lot—probably too much—rides on the results of these tests for individuals and schools. If they could be quickly constructed, administered, and graded, they might be efficient, but they would lack acceptable validity and reliability.

When a program is appropriately assessed, the evaluation becomes a matter of integrating the results of the various measures and deciding whether to maintain, revise, or discontinue it.

Before any decisive evaluation, it is critical to gather sufficient assessment data, using multiple measures over a period of time. Programs have been evaluated out of existence without allowing adequate time for significant changes; substantial curriculum innovations require months, even years, for teachers to become comfortable with them, and for students to learn. In complex subjects like reading or writing, stable and enduring improvements usually come about only over lengthy interventions.

Often, other issues need to be considered before any action is taken. If revisions are needed, who will do what, when, and how much will it cost? If the program is demonstrably successful, how will this information be disseminated to all parties of interest? If it is unsuccessful, and no remediation appears possible, why did it fail, and what will take its place?

Steps in the Evaluation Process

Begin by answering the question: "How will we use the results of the evaluation?" For "low stakes" decisions—minor program adjustments, or those with a modest impact on a single class—consider these steps:

1. Define the purposes of the program; what measurable outcomes will indicate the goals have been achieved?

2. Assess the status of the class on the knowledge and skills the program targets before intervention began.
3. Assess the status of the class after the program has operated enough time to permit change to take place.
4. Evaluate the change, that is, the difference between 2 and 3 above. Does the change indicate that the program is successful? Does it suggest helpful modifications?

Note: In verifying pre- and post-assessment outcomes one should use all available quantitative and qualitative measures. Well-designed tests offer objective, quantifiable data, but qualitative indicators such as teachers' observations and checklists, and attitudes of students, colleagues, and parents about the program can contribute constructively to a decision.

For high-stakes evaluations—judgments about programs whose outcomes are of critical importance and whose evaluations require a substantial outlay of resources—the process resembles that for low-stakes evaluations, but each of the steps must be much more thorough:

1. Because the decisions stemming from the evaluation may significantly impact students and teachers and affect the allocation of resources, evaluators should try to inform and involve all parties of interest in the program about the plans, processes, and outcomes of the evaluation.
2. Define and obtain consensus on the program's intended outcomes; in a post-intervention evaluation, note possible unintended outcomes that may have surfaced.
3. State the intended use of the evaluation results. Be certain that those who have the authority for a final decision, for example, school board members, understand the potential consequences of the evaluation results.
4. Formulate and disseminate an evaluation plan that covers the three points above, and includes as well a timeline, the persons to be involved, the needed resources, the applicable assessment techniques, and the reporting and decision-making process.

SUMMARY

- Assessment, or data gathering, is distinct from evaluation, which interprets the data and uses it to make decisions.
- The key question: "How will we use the results of an evaluation?"
- Formative evaluation uses numerous assessments, some quite informal, to diagnose how well students are learning. Summative evaluation is more rigorous, because the results may initiate major decisions about curriculum.

- Well-designed tests are an important source of information in evaluating curriculum. However, the test data should be supplemented by other assessment methods.
- The principal qualities of an assessment-evaluation are: validity, reliability, and efficiency.

Chapter 9

What Works?

Chapters four through seven describe some 27 schools and three districts that vary widely in the readiness of their students to learn, but which have all been successful in raising and maintaining a high level of student achievement.

The schools and districts profiled in this book were chosen from some 80 successful schools we investigated, primarily by accessing the schools' own websites and those of various organizations that investigate and describe high-performing schools. (See Internet Websites for information from and about those organizations.)

Predictably, the interventions that work for schools with a seriously disadvantaged population are not always the strategies chosen for a more privileged student body. Still, some commonalities emerge between schools for the poor and those for the more privileged. In this chapter, we will highlight those common themes.

Common Elements

The first general characteristic of successful schools is that their administrators and teachers are committed to *not* doing business as usual. These educators undertake an intensive study of their own students' needs. Then they choose curriculum content and teaching strategies that seem appropriate to those needs. Next they undergo the training they need to try out the new approaches, assess and evaluate the results, then refine the programs.

A second practice that is common to successful schools is the formulation of clear rules for student behavior, including attendance, attention to classroom instruction, and homework. Such a code of behavior works when it has the support of faculty, parents, and the students themselves.

Attitudes, Practices, and Policies

1. As mentioned above, the primary requisite for successful curriculum revision is a *willingness and ability to change* on the part of the faculty. Experienced teachers don't always find it easy to "go back to school," and learn new approaches to course content and instructional methodologies. Some assume that a request to do so means that they've not been doing a good job, and their current teaching is unsatisfactory. Unfortunately, that is sometimes true, but none of us likes to face such a criticism. A willingness to learn new methods is important but, as indicated in item five below, a carefully designed, cooperative approach to professional development is critical for moving from "I'm willing to change" to "I know how to change."

2. High, appropriate *expectations* for student progress are essential. Three conditions are especially important for such expectations: first, the course content is challenging in relation to students' current knowledge and skills. There is no point in touting a "rigorous curriculum" for students who lack the necessary background in the subject. Schools and districts that are teaching algebra in ever earlier grades are seeing their well-prepared students soar ahead in mathematics, but increasingly, students who lack a thorough grounding in arithmetic are adrift in algebra class. Especially in mathematics, learning difficulties are sure to follow if students who lack the information and skills for more demanding courses are moved ahead prematurely.

    A second requirement if high expectations are to be attainable is frequent formative assessment. Several factors have conflated to make formative classroom assessment less frequent than it should be. This situation is due, at least in part, to the feelings of many teachers that assessments, especially those mandated by the state, are unproductive burdens on both teachers and students. The practice of frequent classroom assessments needs to be rehabilitated if teachers are to determine what their students have learned, and what they are ready to learn next. These assessments may include occasional written tests that are formal and comprehensive, but more often consist of brief, informal checks on student progress.

    The third requirement for meeting high expectations is prompt support for those students who are faltering. When assessments show that a class or some students within a class are not grasping the essentials of a course, it is unconscionable simply to assign a low grade and move on. In schools that are successfully using Response to Intervention (RTI), for example, students receive prompt help that is gradually intensified according to individual students' needs.

3. A practice that characterizes virtually all successful schools is a laser-like focus on *language*. Especially for ESL students, that concentration includes speaking and understanding spoken English as well as reading and writing. At all levels of schooling, for students whose family backgrounds do not facilitate learning English, schools make intensive efforts to improve their students' communication skills. These efforts are most prevalent in the early elementary years, where teachers adapt the usual content and teaching methods to their students' learning status and needs. In middle and high schools that serve disadvantaged populations, once basic grammar and vocabulary are in place, students' reading and writing instruction proceeds to more complex literature and to greater fluency and style in writing and speaking. Nevertheless, some students fall through the cracks in elementary school language learning, so some middle and high school programs include opportunities for basic language instruction taught by reading specialists.

4. A policy of successful schools is a requirement that teachers follow a *sequence of instruction* that coordinates with other classes at the same grade levels, and allows teachers to know, at the beginning of each school year, what their incoming students have studied. The need to cover material likely to occur in state standards-based assessment can motivate teachers and administrators to adopt a uniform content and schedule, but even without that stimulus, teachers and students benefit from a curriculum that is known and followed. This uniformity in content and schedule ought not inhibit teachers from deciding on the teaching strategies that seem most appropriate for their students, or from supplementing the standardized curriculum.

5. Successful schools emphasize the *professional development* of their staffs. A school's teaching staff is its principal resource; a professional development program that teachers and administrators develop cooperatively recognizes that fact. Such programs offer repeated opportunities during the school year for reviews of the curriculum and student progress as well as the development of new knowledge and teaching skills. But professional development is still something of an afterthought in many U.S. schools.

6. In a given year, only about one percent of the teaching force enters the profession from teacher education programs. It seems sensible to devote

a great deal of planning and resources to improving the knowledge and skills of the 99 percent who are in-service teachers.

Several schools profiled in this text are making rapidly increasing commitments of funds and time to improving both the amount and the quality of in-service education. These schools have moved from the familiar one- to two-day workshop once or twice a year to cooperative needs assessments. Once students' status and needs are indentified, a sustained commitment to devising classroom strategies follows, new approaches are tried, the results discussed, and successful strategies are adopted into the curriculum.

This approach to teacher learning reflects practices in other countries like Finland and Singapore that record high levels of student achievement. For years, many U.S. educators comforted themselves with the belief that students who score high in international assessments, especially in Asian countries, do so because, "They just memorize and drill."

In fact, those school systems understand the importance of teaching problem solving and critical thinking; they also recognize that for children to learn complex skills, those entering teaching must be among their most capable young people. Having attracted promising candidates to teaching, these societies invest heavily in their training throughout the teachers' careers. The success these nations enjoy in upgrading their schools is surely due in large measure to their dedicating substantial resources to teacher pre- and in-service education.

7. Successful schools at every level strive to gain the *support of students' families.* A lack of parental support is a complaint commonly heard in faculty rooms. As we indicate in chapter three, parental interest and backing is almost a given in affluent communities. It's true that occasionally, the support can become obtrusive and burdensome to teachers and administrators, but generally, such parents are forthcoming with the financial and moral support that schools need.

8. In deeply impoverished communities, when parents do not respond to school communications or attend parents' nights, it is wrong to impute to those parents a lack of concern for their children. Such problems as language and cultural differences, working hours, and child care all contribute to isolating these families from the school. But when their children have a chance to move from a failing school environment to one promising greater success, long lines of would-be registrants appear, and waiting lists far exceed the number of places available.

Some schools successfully reach out to disadvantaged parents by accommodating the schools' contacts to the needs of the parents. See, for example, the programs in the profiles of Westbury Middle School and the Brownsville School district.

The six elements common to successful schools described above do not exhaust the factors that contribute to strong student achievement. Briefly, several others are:

- Leadership, especially that of the local principal: most of the elements for success depend on systematic, sustained coordination among teachers and provision of the time and financial resources they require.
- Continuity in attendance: in our poorest schools, the daily absentee rate may exceed 25 percent. Also, students who change schools usually suffer from breaks in their curriculum. As Woody Allen says, "Ninety percent of the job is just showing up." School learning requires more than students' bodily presence, but without it, learning can't occur.
- Resources: certainly, financial support is important; the more disadvantaged the population, the greater the need for tutoring, additional class days, smaller classes, and other expensive resources. But the key resource is skilled teachers committed to curricula that work for their students. That's why successful schools here and abroad are pouring more time and money into upgrading their teachers' pre- and in-service development programs. Their leaders and teachers know that for their students failure cannot be an option; these educators understand that a well-educated citizenry is essential to maintaining a just and productive society.

SCHOOL TURNAROUNDS

U. S. Secretary of Education, Arne Duncan, has promised that a substantial portion of the $4.35 billion allocated to the Race to the Top project will be devoted to reforming schools whose students are failing to make adequate academic progress. Duncan identifies some 5,000 schools that he terms the nation's worst-performing schools, those most in need of intensive remediation.

Several institutions and projects are developing studies or starting school turnaround projects, according to an article in *Education Week* (Viadero, Aug. 9, 2009). Reforming failing schools is the major intent of the No Child Left Behind Act, and federal and state education departments continue to encourage improvement in schools found to be making less than adequate yearly progress. One program that works toward that end is the Talent Development model that originates at Johns Hopkins University. Another such program is

Success for All, devised by Robert Slavin, also at Johns Hopkins University. The Education Week article also refers to the use, in some schools, of the Direct Instruction model. This approach has been successful in schools whose students are seriously deficient in basic skills, and/or attention.

A principal source for studies that will lead to turnaround projects are schools that are now successful in raising student achievement in severely impoverished communities; it is in these communities that schools and students are most conspicuously failing. Major sections of this book profile such successful schools (chapters 4-7), and chapter 9 distills "what works" from the successful models.

Two other current efforts to encourage school turnaround are Practice Guides, and the School Turnaround Specialist Program. The Practice Guides are produced by the Institute of Educational Sciences, a division of the U.S. Office of Education. The guides focus on specific school problems, such as low student achievement or dropouts; they present data on the problems, and recommend ways of attacking them.

A second, more hands-on approach is that of the School Turnaround Specialist Program at the University of Virginia. This two-year project brings together administrators from school districts and specialists in changing organizational behavior. The specialists are drawn primarily from the University's Darden School of Business and its Curry School of Education. (See the Website, School Turnaround Specialist Program). But the UVA program also relies heavily on school administrators and teachers who have demonstrated an ability to raise the achievement of seriously disadvantaged students.

Urban communities with at least some schools that now show positive results in raising student achievement include Philadelphia, Boston, Chicago, New York, and Hartford, Connecticut. As these successes, as well as those mentioned in this text become better known and lessons derived from them become systematically disseminated, we see hope for a turnaround in schools that are now failing a large percentage of American young people.

Glossary

Accountability: the complete and accurate reporting of goals, procedures, and results of assessment and evaluation.

Anecdotal Record: a description of a performance; it should interpret or score the performance and describe circumstances that influence the performance.

Assessment: gathering and organizing data to measure performance.

Average Score: the sum of all scores divided by the number of scores; also termed the *mean*.

Behavioral Objectives: statements of the performance to be measured, the conditions of the performance, and the level required for mastery.

Classroom Assessments: the various forms of student assessments chosen or created by classroom teachers.

Core Knowledge Curriculum: a sequence of basic knowledge and skills organized by subject and grade level for elementary and middle school students.

Criterion-Referenced Assessment: measures the degree of mastery for a given body of knowledge or skills.

Differentiated Instruction: adjusts curriculum content and instructional strategies to diagnosed needs of individual and groups of students.

Efficiency: the balance between the time and effort required to prepare, administer, and score assessments, and an adequate sampling of the domain being sampled.

English as a Second Language (ESL): for students whose native and home language is not English; such students are also termed English Language Learners (ELL), or Limited English Proficient (LEP).

Evaluation: a judgment based on the results of assessment.

Formative Evaluation: the use of assessment results for advising and supporting student learning, or modifying lesson plans.

Free/Reduced-Fee Lunch: provided for children of families with income at or below 130 percent of the poverty level.

Grade-Equivalent Scores: the average level of performance for every month at every grade level. A grade-equivalent of 6.3 is the level of an average student in the third month of grade six.

Grade Point Average: the average of student grades over a given period; it is calculated by assigning a value of 4 to an A, 3 to a B, 2 to a C, 1 to a D, and 0 to an F.

Item Analysis: each student's responses to every question on a test; it also gives the correct answer, how many students chose correctly, and the number of students in a class who chose each other response.

Norm-Referenced Scores: test-takers' performance in relation to a specified group of students.

Objectives: the intended results of instruction. They should be stated in measurable terms to permit an assessment of performance.

Outcomes: like objectives, they are the measurable results of instruction.

Percentile Band: a range within which the "true score" falls. It recognizes that every test is subject to errors of measurement.

Percentile Rank: the score below which a given percentage of students in the group falls. A student's percentile rank will vary depending on the ability of the norms group with which it is compared.

Rating Scales: provide categories that allow an observer to indicate the degree of competency an individual demonstrates.

Reliability: the consistency of results for an assessment, an individual, or a group of test-takers.

Response to Intervention (RTI): a program that adapts instruction to the needs of individual students; for struggling students, the program begins with standard classroom, then moves to tutoring, interventions by specialists, and full-scale assessments for possible special education placement.

Standard Error of Measurement: the extent to which scores would differ if test-takers were re-tested with different questions that measure the same knowledge and skills at the same level of difficulty.

Standardized Test: an assessment designed to measure specific content and standards, with detailed protocols for administering and scoring the test, and interpreting the results.

Summative Evaluation: a judgment based on the assessment of overall performance of a program or of individuals in relation to specific objectives.

Validity: the extent to which an assessment measures what it claims to measure. A measure is valid in relation to the intended use of the assessment results.

Internet Websites for Successful Schools

We found the organizations listed below most helpful among the many devoted to recognizing schools that significantly raise students' academic achievement.

Specific websites (www. etc.) are easily miscopied, so we simply list the organizations' names. When the names are entered in Google Search or another internet search service, an array of websites and links will appear.

In seeking information about a specific school or district, enter the school or district name and the city or state in which it is located.

Accelerated Schools Project (Center at Teachers College, Columbia University)

Achieve, Inc. (Focuses on standard setting and testing)

Best Evidence Encyclopedia (Reviews of research at all levels of schooling)

Broad Prize Awards (School districts best serving severely disadvantaged students)

Center for Data Driven Reform in Education (Johns Hopkins School of Education: research and dissemination of proven strategies)

Center for Public Education (Research findings, best practices)

Effective Schools (Association for Effective Schools)

Great Schools (Nationwide ratings and descriptions)

High Schools that Work (Southern Regional Education Board: initiatives to improve middle schools and high schools)

National Center for Educational Accountability (Best practices)

National Center for Educational Achievement (Best practices, case studies)

National Center for Educational Statistics (A compilation of information on the condition of education in the U.S.)

Partnership for 21st Century Skills (A framework of student outcomes and support systems)

School Turnaround Specialist Program (Two year program for school administrators at the University of Virginia)

Successful Elementary (Middle, High) Schools

What Works Clearinghouse (U.S. Office of Education, American Institute for Research)

References and Bibliography

Anderson, L. W. & Krathwohl, D. R. (Eds.) (2001). *A taxonomy for learning, teaching, and assessing: A revision of Bloom's taxonomy of educational objectives* (Complete ed.). Boston: Allyn & Bacon.

Anderson, R. C. & Shifrin, Z. (1980). The meaning of words in context. In R. T. Spiro, et al.

Brewer, W. (Ed.) (1980). *Theoretical issues in reading comprehension.* Hillsdale, NJ: Lawrence Erlbaum Associates.

Barton, P. & Coley, R. (2008). *Windows on achievement and inequality.* Princeton, NJ: Policy Evaluation and Research Center, Educational Testing Service.

Beland, K. (2007, April). Boosting social and emotional competencies. *Educational Leadership, 64* (7), pp. 68–71.

Bereiter, C. & Engleman, S. (1966). *Teaching disadvantaged children in the preschool.* Englewood Cliffs, NJ: Prentice-Hall.

Berliner, D. C. (2009). *Poverty and potential: Out-of-school factors and school success.* Boulder & Tempe: Education and the Public Interest Center and the Public Interest Center and Education Policy Unit.

Bestor, A. (1953, 2nd ed. 1985). *Educational wastelands.* Champaign, IL: University of Illinois Press.

Blackburn, B. (2008). *Rigor is not a four letter word.* Larchmont, NY: Eye on Education.

Blankstein, A. (Ed.) (2004). *Failure is not an option: How high-achieving districts succeed with all students* (3 vols.). Thousand Oaks, CA: Corwin Press.

Breland, H. M., Jones, R. J., & Jenkins, L. (1994). *The College Board vocabulary study.* New York: College Board Publications.

California Department of Education (2001). *Introduction to history – Social science content standards.* Sacramento, CA.

Center for American Progress and Institute for America's Future (2005). *Getting smarter, becoming fairer: A progressive education agenda for a stronger nation.* Washington, DC: Author.

Coleman, J. S. (1991). *Parental involvement in education.* Washington, DC: U. S. Department of Education.

Cremin, L. A. (1961). *The transformation of the school: Progressivism in American education, 1865–1967.* New York: Knopf Doubleday.

Council for Basic Education (1998). *Standards for excellence in education.* Washington, DC: Author.

Doljes, C. (2006, October). *Report on key practices and policies of consistently higher performing high schools.* Washington, DC: National High School Center, American Institute for Research.

Dweck, C. S. (2006). *Mindset: The new psychology of success.* New York: Random House.

Edmonds, R. R. (1979, October). Effective schools for the urban poor. *Educational Leadership, 37* (1), pp. 15–18, 20–24.

Education Trust (2005). *Gaining traction, gaining ground: How some high schools accelerate learning for struggling students.* Washington, DC: Author.

English, F. & Steffy, B. (2001). *Deep curriculum alignment.* Lanham, MD: Scarecrow Press.

English, F. (2000). *Deciding what to teach and test: Developing, aligning, and auditing the curriculum.* Thousand Oaks, CA: Corwin Press.

Fadiman, C. (1959). *The case for basic education.* (James D. Koerner, ed.). Boston: Little, Brown, & Co.

Finn, C. & Meier, D. (2009, Spring). E pluribus unum? *Education Next, 9* (2), p. 55.

Flood, J., Lapp, D., Squires, D. J., & Jensen, J. M. (Eds.). *Handbook of research in teaching the English language arts* (2nd ed. pp. 799–813). Mahwah, NJ: Lawrence Erlbaum Associates.

Frey, N., Fisher, D., & Moore, K. (2005). *Designing responsive curriculum: Planning lessons that work.* Lanham, MD: Rowman and Littlefield Education.

Garcia, E. E., Scribner, K., & Jensen, B. (2009, April). The demographic imperative. *Educational Leadership, 66* (7), pp. 8–13.

Gootman, E. (2008, August 26). 10 city schools to focus reading skills on content. *The New York Times,* p. B3.

Goldin, C. & Katz, L. F. (2008). *The race between education and technology.* Cambridge: Belknap Press.

Gordon, E. B., Morgan, R., O'Malley, C., & Porticelli, J. (2006). *The tutoring revolution: Applying research for best practices, policy implications, and student achievement.* Lanham, MD: Rowman and Littlefield Education.

Greene, S. P. & Winters, M. A. (2006). The effects of residential school choice on public high school graduation rates. *Peabody Journal of Education:* 81 (1).

Hart, B. & Risley, T. R. (2003, Spring). The early catastrophe: The 30 million word gap by age 3. *American Educator.* Vol. 27, No. 1

Hirsch, E. D. Jr. (1987). *Cultural literacy: What every American needs to know.* Boston: Houghton Mifflin.

——— (2006). *The knowledge deficit: Closing the shocking education gap for American children.* Boston: Houghton Mifflin.

Hord, S. M. (2008). *Leading professional learning communities: Voices from research and practice.* Thousand Oaks, CA: Corwin Press.

Human Resources Research Organization (2007, October). *Behind the numbers: Interviews in 22 states about achievement data and No Child Left Behind Act policies* (Phase 2 Report). Washington, DC: Center on Education Policy.

Jossey-Bass (2001). *The Jossey-Bass reader on school reform.* San Francisco: Jossey-Bass.

Leithwood, K., Jantzi, D., & Aitlen, R. (2006). *Making school smarter* (3rd ed.). Thousand Oaks, CA: Corwin Press.

Marzano, R. J., Pickering, D., & Pollock, J. (2001). *Classroom instruction that works: Research-based strategies for increasing student achievement.* Alexandria, VA: Association for Supervision and Curriculum Development.

Marzano, R. J. (2004). *Building background knowledge for academic achievement.* Alexandria, VA: Association for Supervision and Curriculum Development.

Mathews, J. (2009). *Work hard, be nice.* Chapel Hill, NC: Algonquin Books.

National Assessment of Educational Progress (2007). *America's high school graduates: Results from the 2005 NAEP high school transcript study.* (Electronic version). Retrieved from www.nces.ed.gov/nationsreportcard/hsts.

Nordlund, M. (2003). *Differentiated instruction: Meeting the educational needs of all students in your classroom.* Lanham, MD: Rowman and Littlefield.

Ouchi, W. (2003). *Making schools work.* New York: Simon & Schuster.

Ruddell, M. R. (1993). *Teaching content reading and writing.* Boston: Allyn & Bacon.

Shepard, L. (1993). *Setting performance standards for student achievement: A report of the national academy of education panel on the evaluation of the NAEP trial state assessment.* Stanford, CA: National Academy of Education, Stanford University.

Slavin, R. E. & Madden, N. (1996). *Every child, every school: Success for all.* Thousand Oaks, CA: Corwin Press.

Smith, J. R., Brooks-Gunn, J., & Klebanov, P. K. (1997). Consequences of living in poverty for young children's cognitive and verbal ability and early school achievement. In Duncan, G. J., & Brooks-Gunn, J. *Consequences of growing up poor.* New York: Russell Sage Foundation.

Snow, C., Griffin, P., & Burns, M. S. (Eds.) (2007). *Knowledge to support the teaching of reading.* San Francisco: Jossey-Bass.

Stiggins, Rick. (May 2009). Maximizing the power of formative assessments. *Phi Delta Kappan,* (pp. 640–644).

Taba, H. (1962). *Curriculum development: Theory and practice.* New York: Harcourt Brace.

Tough, P. (2008). *Whatever it takes.* Boston: Houghton-Mifflin.

Tyler, R. (1949). *Basic principles of curriculum and instruction.* Chicago: University of Chicago Press.

Viadero, Debra. (2009, August 12). Research doesn't offer much guidance on turnarounds. *Education Week,* p. 10. Vol. 28, No. 37

Vygotsky, L. S. (1976). *Thought and language.* Cambridge, MA: MIT Press.

Wiggins, G. & McTighe, J. (1998). *Understanding by design.* Alexandria, VA: Association for Supervision and Curriculum Development.

Willingham, D. (2009). *Why students don't like school.* San Francisco: Wiley, Jossey-Bass.

Wilson, J. W. (1987). *The truly disadvantaged: The inner-city, the underclass, and public policy.* Chicago: University of Chicago Press.

Wortham, S. C. (2008). *Assessment of early childhood education* (4th ed.). Upper Saddle River, NJ: Pearson Education.

Zakaria, F. (2008). *The post-American world.* New York: W. W. Norton.

About the Author

James Deneen is retired from Educational Testing Service, where he was a program director for the Advanced Placement Program and for Teacher Programs and Services. Earlier, he was a teacher and school administrator in K–12 schools, and taught school administration at the University of Toronto's Graduate School of Education. He has written some 40 books and articles, principally on educational assessment, and has presented numerous workshops on that topic. He coauthored with Chris Deneen a text on assessing student achievement, published in 2008 by Rowman and Littlefield Education. Jim received his Ph.D. in school administration from Indiana University.